CW00747470

# LOOKING FOR NORMAL

## AUTISM AND OTHER COMPLICATED STUFF

### STEVE SLAVIN

MARSHWOOD

*For Bonnie.*

# CONTENTS

INTRODUCTION vii

1. TELLING DAD: 2008 1
2. AUTISM STREET 4
3. EARLY YEARS: 1959 10
4. A LITTLE HISTORY 15
5. SCHOOL AND OTHER NIGHTMARES 23
6. MR WILLIAMS 26
7. BRADLEY DAVIES 32
8. THE ONSET OF OCD 35
9. GRASMERE AVENUE 42
10. GRANDPA 47
11. A TEAM OF ONE 54
12. A NEW DECADE 58
13. HOSPITAL: 1970 61
14. MONKTON WYLD 66
15. THE IMPORTANCE OF MUSIC 82
16. LEARNING THE PIANO: 1971 85
17. HOW I BECAME GEORGE: 1972 90
18. LEARNING THE GUITAR: 1972 95
19. GOLF: MY OCD HELL 102
20. GOLF: THE PATH TO ENLIGHTENMENT 108
21. IN HOSPITAL AGAIN: 1972 114
22. SCANDAL 121
23. THE AUTISTIC HIPPIE 124
24. DAVE 128
25. FIRST LOVE: JANUARY 1976 133
26. AFTER MONKTON 139
27. FUNK AND FINE FABRICS: 1978 148

28. HOWARD AND ME: 1980     161

29. SORRY, I CAN'T REMEMBER     169

30. THE BEES: 1981     176

31. THE STRANGEST LOVE OF ALL: 1982     187

32. AD2000: 1982     199

33. BONNIE: 1984     203

34. FINDING MY IDENTITY     208

35. SUCCESS AT LAST: 1986     218

36. SEPTEMBER 1987     225

37. CILLA AND THE FRISBEE     231

38. AFTER THE APOCALYPSE: 1990     241

39. OCD AND THE MILLENNIUM BUG     251

40. THE IMPOSSIBLE ART OF CONVERSATION     257

41. HUGO: 2005     264

42. IMPOSTER SYNDROME     271

43. STEVE THE VIDEO GUY: 2006     277

44. LOST IN TRANSLATION.     286

45. THE DIAGNOSIS: 2008     289

46. 2008     301

47. WHAT IS NORMAL ANYWAY?     305

48. IN CONCLUSION     313

Acknowledgments     315

# INTRODUCTION

Why is a book about my autism diagnosis at 48 years of age entitled *Looking for Normal?*

Well, after much procrastination, I decided, finally, that *Looking for Normal* best conveys the irony, humour and poignancy with which I tell my story.

Other titles I considered were:

*People*: *A Beginners Guide for The Socially Dyslexic.*

This has a certain ring to it, but it only relates to a part of my story. I have left this idea to simmer gently on the literary back-burner for another day.

I also considered the title:

*Autism And Other Complicated Stuff I Was Too Embarrassed to Talk About—But Did Anyway.*

This, I decided, was both accurate and mildly humorous, but a little too long.

Once, when going through a particularly angry phase, I considered calling my book:

*What...? I'm Autistic? Why the Hell Didn't My Overpaid, Under-Educated Psychiatrist Tell Me this Forty-Years Ago?*

I dismissed this idea on the grounds that I didn't want to come across all bitter and twisted. Or, at least admit publicly, that I was, in fact—all bitter and twisted.

I also toyed with the idea of calling this book:

*Can I Start Again Please?*

This title has a lot going for it. It's relatively concise, and expresses with clarity, my fanciful desire to restart the clock at 1959 and do it all again—but this time as a knowingly autistic person.

Other difficult questions arise when writing such deeply personal accounts for public consumption.

For example: how much navel-gazing is acceptable in a memoir before one's words are dismissed as unattractive narcissism? And just *when,* exactly*,* does helpful introspection morph into tedious self-indulgence?

I hope that readers will feel I've struck a happy balance in my attempt at elucidation. And perhaps some may even benefit from the warm comfort of the odd shared experience.

Writing a memoir is, it turns out, not dissimilar to instigating an extraordinarily embarrassing conversation about stuff you'd rather not discuss—with strangers that may not be in the slightest bit interested in anything you have to say.

For now, however, I shall endeavour to ignore my insecurities, and submit my tale of life, autism, and all the other complicated stuff I didn't want to talk about —but have, anyway.

Happy reading

*Steven*

# TELLING DAD: 2008

*There's something about a crisis that allows us to visit that rare space, where uncommon truth meets all that is best in us—and there is no crisis greater than the impending death of a loved one.*

'But you *can't* be autistic; you're way too smart. Look at all the amazing things you can do!'

I sat opposite my disbelieving father in the hospital café, just a short walk from where mum lay comatose, and in her final days.

'Well, dad, it's like *this*,' I continued to explain awkwardly…

'Autism happens on a kind of spectrum. It means that I get lost a lot when I'm driving, and I hate being in noisy places.'

'But doesn't *everyone* get lost sometimes?' Dad countered with unquestionable logic.

'Well, yes, of course,' I replied, struggling to put a medical slant on traits experienced by most people at some point in their lives.

'Look, dad, autism is a complex thing, I'm not exactly sure what it all means yet, or how to describe it, I just know I *have* it. My psychologist has done all the tests and confirmed everything in writing.'

It had, in fact, been three months since Dr C delivered her game-changing, clinical conclusion. Yet, until that afternoon in late September 2008, I had regarded any discussion with dad concerning my *problematic* childhood, as being strictly out of bounds, taboo, and definitely *not* up for debate.

But now as the days began to shorten into mum's final autumn, the time felt *right* to dispense with my embarrassment, and admit to him that his son was, without a shadow of a doubt, *autistic*.

Our second round of tasteless hospital coffee arrived as the light began to fade through the large café windows. And with the exception of an exhausted nurse on a tea break, dad and I were alone in a perfect moment—spoiled only by the sound of clattering cutlery and a beeping microwave timer.

I watched the waitress clear the tables of empty white coffee cups for the final time that day, and realised that, regardless of one's personal circumstances, tables still need to be cleaned, and floors swept of the days discarded remains.

'We're closing in five-minutes,' shouted the waitress abruptly without stopping to look up. 'We'd better go before she throws us out!' I said to dad with a wry half-smile, and followed dad along the corridor to the ward where mum lay motionless—somewhere in that unreachable place between sleep and a deeper unconsciousness.

'Goodnight mum…' I whisper gently, leaving a soft kiss on her forehead. 'We've got to go now. I'll come and see you again tomorrow.'

At forty-eight years of age I was about to lose a mother, but in my father, gain a surprisingly empathetic new friend.

## 2

## AUTISM STREET

*I would like to walk along Autism Street where everyone goes in the same direction as me.*

*On Autism Street, pedestrians would travel along tracks with predetermined routes from which they could not stray.*

*Police sirens would be silent on Autism Street and their flashing lights dimmed to a glow.*

*I wish that every pavement was free from the clutter of humans and their chatter on phones— just like the one on Autism Street.*

Imagine this: You're in a busy high street. You see the wheel of a car, someone's arm, a reflection from a shop window, a discarded coffee cup.

This is my world. A world of unconnected bits of *things* and dots that cannot be joined.

Life, for me, is a random collection of unsettling

emotions caused by fleeting pictures. None of which relate to each other—or to *me.*

My differently wired brain robs me of the ability to see the *whole* picture. Instead, I see life through the lens of a telescope—a tightly cropped perspective that ignores the broader context.

The name of this particular aspect of the autistic condition is *Weak Central Coherence.* A term coined by the ground-breaking autism researcher *Dr Uta Frith* in 1989. Her Weak Central Coherence theory explains why people with autism struggle to integrate all the necessary bits of information into a single unified whole.

But, what does this mean in practical terms?

Well, a friend recently described my problem-solving skills like this:

'Steve is more likely to spend all day earnestly scratching a hole in a brick wall with his fingernails to form an exit, than he is to realise he can simply walk through the open door like everyone else.'

Yes, if I'm famous for anything, it's my legendary ability to miss the *obvious* at every possible opportunity*, and*, in the above analogy, a simple solution to a simple problem.

Although seeing the world through such a tiny lens has its occasional benefits, generally, these do not offset the challenges we face.

Let me tell you about an acquaintance of mine. I'll call him *Bob,* a stereotypical Aspergian geek who writes computer software for a living. Bob locks himself away for hours on end, perfecting every single line of code as if his life depended on it. And whilst he may be unusually gifted in this area, every other aspect of his life is best described as *chaotic*.

Bob is unable to form friendships and finds it excruciatingly uncomfortable to sustain more than a few seconds of continuous eye-contact. This, however, suits his co-workers fine. They know that if he *does* catch their eye for even a second, he's likely to bombard them with a-hundred-and-one facts about some obscure 1980s cartoon character, or his other passion: *London buses 1987-2017.* Bob is rarely seen without the battered briefcase containing his entire picture collection of London double-deckers—each one meticulously catalogued by route, number, and date of manufacture.

Bob tells me that the number *67* from Parsons Avenue, *actually* used to travel along Heath Road. But due to the recent cutbacks, this route is now covered by the number *75* that only stops on weekdays between the hours of 10 am and 4 pm.

I'm often tempted to say, 'hmm… that's *fascinating* Bob,' but this would only encourage a further onslaught of interesting facts relating to the *34* from Vicarage Lane to Waverley Gardens, and the extra three-minutes of journey time caused by that new one-way system in Windsor Drive.

Bob finds comfort and certainty in the detailed

structure of *things,* and in facts, figures, and the predictability of inanimate objects.

Like me, Bob's tendency to become lost in the very *small*, far outweighs his ability to form a useful overview of the very *big*. It's all about perspective, or in my case, the lack of it. Autistic people like us, just can't seem to see past the ends of our noses. If only I could have the grand, all-seeing vision of a *Richard Branson*, or a *Steve Jobs RIP,* for a day—just to see how it felt.

In fact, If I had a pound for every time I heard a neurotypical person say, 'you don't look autistic,' I probably *would* be as wealthy as a Richard Branson or a Steve Jobs RIP.

So, what is it like to see the world through the tiny lens of *Weak Central Coherence?*

- It's like jumping into a lovely patch of warm, blue water without noticing the circling family of sharks two feet away.

- It's like looking into a bowl filled with fruit of all kinds, and seeing only the oranges.

- It's like waiting at the bus stop for ages without seeing the unmissable bright red sign that clearly states: *BUS STOP NOT IN*

*USE.* And now you're late for work and getting *really* stressed out.

The autistic condition displays itself as a kind of random hotchpotch of functionality and deficit. Each category of symptoms combining with such complexity, as to create a unique experience for each person on the *spectrum.* And this is *before* we begin to factor in any inherent personality traits that may have existed had that person *not* been autistic.

So, getting back to Bob. Despite his remarkable ability in the field of computing, his social skills are poor. I, on the other hand, have slightly better social skills, but due to more pronounced cognitive dysfunction in other areas, do not share Bob's ability to remember facts and figures. I also have zero interest in London buses—other than the one I've been waiting for at the wrong bus stop, and on the wrong side of the street, in the rain, for over an hour.

I do not process speech and language very well, and neither does Bob, but for different reasons. He is able to *catch* every word he hears but will misunderstand the context. Whereas, I can usually judge the context, but remain hopeless at retaining any information in the first place. This means our conversation's do not have the usual ebb and flow of an average *neurotypical* interaction. We talk *at* each other for a couple of confusing minutes with virtually zero eye-contact, and then he's gone—without a goodbye, or a *see you later*.

A conversation with Bob may go something like this:

*Me—'hi Bob, how are you today?'*

*Bob—'did you know that Captain Kirk's kiss with Lieutenant Uhura on the Starship Enterprise in 1968 was the first interracial kiss on TV?'*

*Me—'umm… can you repeat that please, I can't remember what you said?'*

*Bob—'I must be going now.'*

*Me—'oh… Ok then, goodbye Bob.'*

We may share a diagnosis, yet we are different in every other conceivable way.

I can totally understand why some people think Bob and I are just a little bit different to *them*, and also to each other. But then, everyone on planet autism is—just a little bit different to everyone else.

## 3

### EARLY YEARS: 1959

*'From the moment you were born, all you did was scream. You'd not eat, and you wouldn't sleep. No one knew what was wrong with you!'*

Home in 1959, was a two-bedroom maisonette above a row of shops in West London—Ealing Broadway to be precise. And for this humble abode, dad paid the hefty sum of £1800—a fair size mortgage when your weekly wage is £8.

Shortly after settling in, the bulldozers arrived to flatten the surrounding area to make way for the new underpass. And this—mum was convinced—was the reason for my *extreme nervousness* as a child. Two years later, she'd thought my sister's somewhat protracted birth, had been caused by an exploding truck a few streets away.

It's not unreasonable to suppose that mum's theories on road noise and childbirth may have held some scientific merit, but mum was a woman driven by paranormal tinged instinct, and not by science—she just always seemed to *know* stuff...

'I knew you were going to be a boy, *and,* that I would call you *Steven*,' she once told me.

Apparently, shortly before I was born, a man in a brown, pinstriped suit had come to her in a dream and said she would give birth to a male child. The child should be named after him.

The mysterious man in the dream turned out to be her mother *Sadie's* dead brother *Sam*—previously unknown to mum.

And in response to her supernatural visitor's request, she took the letter *S* from his name and called me Steven. Personally, I would have preferred something a little more biblical like Saul, or Solomon. But the thing I hate most about the name *Steven Slavin* is just how incredibly difficult I find it to pronounce. There's simply too many S's and too many V's.

But getting back to the spring of 1959. It soon became clear that mum wasn't coping well with her new child. And so, together we were placed in a mother and baby unit at London's *Great Ormond Street Hospital for Sick Children.* This would provide some much-needed respite for mum, and allow the doctors to investigate my unexplained infantile anxiety.

My earliest memories begin to emerge from the murk of childhood consciousness from around the age of five.

I remember the chronic stomach pain that so frequently forced me to writhe around in agony on my bedroom floor. I remember the tantrums, and being terrified of just about everything, and everyone. I also remember the weekly trips to a nearby clinic where I'd move toys around in a sandpit whilst answering questions posed by a man in a brown tweed jacket. The man was called a speech therapist, and mum said he was going to help me speak. I wasn't exactly sure what *speaking* meant at the time, but according to mum, it was not something I did until year six of my troubled young life.

I also remember my poor, exhausted mother dragging me from clinic to clinic, and from psychologist to psychiatrist. Yet, still, the doctors could not discover what lay behind my emotional instability. They kept saying my stomach pain was something called *psychosomatic*. Adding that my tummy hurt because I'd get so upset and worried about everything.

But why so much fear and anxiety in such a young child? This, no one knew. However, my lack of speech, social anxiety, and general introversion, drove their thinking towards a diagnosis of Childhood

Schizophrenia—a common misdiagnosis at the time for children now considered autistic.

In 1968, the diagnostic mental health guidelines used by clinicians to evaluate their patients—the DSM 2—described schizophrenia as:

*Atypical and withdrawn behaviour, failure to develop an identity separate from the mother, general unevenness, gross immaturity and inadequacy in development.*

The language used in the DSM 2 may hark back to a time when it was acceptable to refer to children like me as abnormal and maladjusted, but I can't deny how well this definition of schizophrenia matched my symptoms.

Mum had also been a victim of the era's flawed thinking—falling unkindly into the category known as the *Refrigerator Mother*.

It was thought that a child's inability to socialise in the normal way was due to a mother's *emotional coldness*. This, in turn, would prevent their child from developing typical social and communication skills.

Whilst a mother's *aloofness* may well inhibit a child's ability to feel empathy, it cannot account for any of autism's genetically derived cognitive differences. I expect there were an entire generation of autism-mothers who carried a heavy burden of guilt to their grave—convinced they were wholly respon-sible for their child's developmental delay.

Thankfully, the archaic Refrigerator Mother theory has long been discarded in the waste bin of clinical thinking.

# 4

## A LITTLE HISTORY

To provide some context for my story, I have decided to share a brief family history. After all, I may have autism, but I am also a product of genetics and environment.

Our family left Russia and Lithuania on boats around 1904. Some went to New York, whilst others came to England. And in the oldest of Jewish traditions, they'd left their homes to escape execution at the hands of yet another murderous regime in need of a scapegoat.

On the plus side, however, necessity has developed in people of this particular faith, the will to succeed, regardless of the circumstances. This remarkable genetic asset takes zero space in a hastily packed suitcase, yet, fills us with such enormous drive and optimism.

And so, from the slums of London's bleak, post-Victorian East End, many of these Eastern European Jews grew their rickety market stalls and backstreet sweatshops into some of the major high street brands we know and love today.

* * *

By his own admission, dad did *not* inherit the brain for business evident in so many of his enterprising Jewish contemporaries. His slow and cautious approach to achieving even moderate financial security was fuelled by a ferocious work ethic, and an admirable conscientiousness. Somehow dad was able to hold down his clothing factory job, work Saturday's in a men's outfitters, decorate the house, and still find time for Sunday afternoon visits to the local park so I could play on the swings.

Still, even with dad working around the clock, money was so tight, that by the end of each month, it was not unusual for supper to consist of a few slices of cheap white bread covered in a thin layer of equally inexpensive strawberry jam.

Mum also had her hands full. She looked after me, my younger sister and the house.

Before I arrived on the scene in the spring of 1959, she had also worked in an East End factory making low-cost clothes for modestly waged women.

Mum's education had been severely interrupted by war. Her years as an evacuee were spent in a village near Peterborough—then a quiet little town of no strategic importance to the Germans.

Yet, still, from the relative safety of her wartime hideaway, mum told me how she would look up from her bedroom window each night to see the British bombers leaving to unload their payloads on Berlin and Dresden. Only to be woken hours later by the ominous drone of returning aircraft—now a sadly depleted squadron limping back to base.

I suspect that even without the upheaval of war, mum would not have been an academic high-flyer, or go-getting tycoon, full of drive and confidence. In any case, expectations for women of her generation did not usually extend beyond that of obedient wife, good mother and efficient house-keeper. And in these tasks, she excelled. Our house was always spotlessly clean, and dinner would appear like clockwork from the stove the moment she heard dad's key turn in the lock at 7 pm each evening.

Yet, although mum always made sure I was dressed as well as money would allow, I could not escape the feeling that something was missing from our relationship. An unexplainable separateness that left me feeling insecure, and, for some inexplicable reason, *guilty*.

It was always the things she *didn't* say that bothered me the most. Her eyes would dart from one thought to the next. Never transforming into words or visible emotion—much like a distant Sun that promised warmth, yet produced little more than a faint glow in an autumn sky.

As a *troubled* child, I wanted her to pick me up and say, *don't worry son, I'll help you get through this, everything's going to be OK.*

But there *were* no reassuring hugs, only words of empty comfort that rang hollow like the cold condolences of a career politician after a disaster of some kind.

Dad's approach to parenting was often a little sterner. 'Come on now Steven, snap out of it,' he'd say, as though I could simply flick a switch in my brain and instantly restore my mood to one of calm normality. But then, in 1960s Britain, the idea of *just getting on with it* was something people generally did.

My pre-teenage years straddled the stoicism of an ageing Victorian generation, and swinging 60s youth culture inspired by The Beatles and the Rolling Stones, Twiggy and Mary Quant.

For the trendy young things of London's Kings Road and Carnaby Street, this may have been the dawning of the age of Aquarius, but for those resting in the quiet conservative shallows of suburbia, life carried on as it had always done—with a stiff-upper-lip, and an equally stiff broom to sweep any uncomfortable truths under one's floral carpet.

In those days, one did not speak publicly about illnesses of the mind. Especially not in Grasmere Avenue where it was practically impossible to contain a rumour once it had leaked beyond your four walls. Social media 1960s style was chatter over the garden fence.

Mum used to say, 'the best way to spread a rumour is to tell Mrs White next door a secret…'

And mum wasn't wrong.

'The Slavin boy is not quite right you know. If he doesn't pull himself together soon they'll lock him away just like they did with that *Johnson* boy a few years ago.'

This was the conversation mum once overheard as she spied on Mrs White, who was spying on *me* whilst gossiping to Ms Spencer two gardens away.

Within days, Mrs White's comments had gone *viral*, and I could sense the judgemental gaze of middle-aged housewives from every aisle as we queued with our basket of essentials in the local supermarket.

'Is Steven poorly Mrs Slavin? Is that why he's off school again?' Someone would ask.

'I hear he's not been coping well.'

'Yes, but he's on the mend now,' mum would fire back irritably. She had long run out of plausible excuses to explain away my frequent absences from school. She was not about to discuss her son's mental health difficulties at the supermarket checkout with someone she barely knew.

'If I wanted everyone to know our business I'd put an advert in the Wembley Gazette!' Mum would mutter defiantly under her breath whilst bagging her modest pile of groceries.

Secretly she was probably thinking how embarrassing it would be if it got out that her child had just been described as, '*maladjusted* and *profoundly disturbed,*' by a crack team of medical experts at Great Ormond Street Hospital.

Who wants their son to be categorised by the locals as being just like *Geoffrey*—the scary *retarded* man that walks past the house each day flapping his hands and talking to himself—always ten steps in front of his ageing mother.

The good folk of Grasmere Avenue would often cross the road whenever they saw Geoffrey and his mother coming along. The commonly held belief appeared to be:

'That man should be in a home with others like him… after all… he could be dangerous!'

I, however, remember feeling an inexplicable empathy with Geoffrey. Somehow, I felt we were cut from the same piece of strange cloth that would forever mark us out as being different.

How times have changed.

In 2018, it's not uncommon to go *public* about a mental health issue or developmental difference. This is generally a good thing. Although, I wonder sometimes if we haven't taken all of this touchy-feely stuff a little too far.

Almost everyone I meet these days has a *syndrome* or a *condition* relating to their emotional health and wellbeing. Celebrities talk openly on TV chat shows about their depression, their addictions and even their sexuality. They are applauded enthusiastically by audiences of sobbing empaths for being so honest, so *human*, and for making the world a better place.

But whilst I generally applaud this type of public testimony, I sometimes wonder if it may also lead to people of the *me too generation* wanting a condition of some kind so they don't feel left out?

And nowadays, people with autism are encouraged to think of themselves as *differently-abled,* rather than to *dis-abled.* This idea may have had some merit if it didn't sound like a strapline concocted in the marketing department of an autism charity. Personally, I hate its empty rhetoric. People on the spectrum need properly funded support, not crappy slogans.

I'm all for inclusiveness—this chimes well with

my hippie ideals. But I worry if the recent outbreak of *Bad-Hair-Day Syndrome* may serve only to trivialise the genuine challenges faced by people with severe mental health conditions and developmental disorders.

## 5

## SCHOOL AND OTHER NIGHTMARES

*Sensory Overload:*

    *The lights that flicker and force my eyes to close. The external noise that explodes my core into cascading shockwaves. The textures that irritate and suffocate every inch of delicate skin.*

It was 7 am on a miserable Monday morning. I stood next to my mother as she did the buttons up on my starched white school shirt. 'You look nice, dear,' she said with the vague hope of encouraging a little happiness in her sobbing son. I may have *looked* nice, but I certainly didn't *feel* very nice. In fact, every inch of that itchy, grey uniform ripped at my skin like a thousand scratchy knives.

She forced a pair of tight black leather shoes over my thick woollen socks. They were the ones I hated with high seams that pushed uncomfortably down onto the tops of my toes. This alone was enough to send me into a violent rage—kicking off my shoes and screaming uncontrollably at the top of my voice.

Mum would disappear for a few minutes then reappeared with a small plate of toasted bread and some warm milk.

'Eat your breakfast *quickly* Steven, we'll have to leave for school soon.'

Feeling too sick and distressed to eat, I'd fall to the floor in despair, whilst wrestling with the hard, irritating edges of my protruding underwear tags.

'Why don't you understand…? I can't go to school…' I'd scream.

'But you *must* go Steven. If you don't, they'll put me in jail and send you away to a special school.'

I'd wedge a pillow between my abdomen and the bedroom floor to ease the stomach ache that would flair-up whenever I was worried about anything.

Eventually, mum would force me out of the house. I'd follow her along Grasmere Avenue and towards the school building, still doubled up in pain and barely able to walk.

\* \* \*

At precisely 8:30 am each morning, the entrance to Preston Park Primary was a chaotic throng of noisy children waving goodbye to their mothers at the school gate. A quick peck on the cheek, and a, '*see you at 3:30 dear*,' and the interaction was complete.

Soon the playground would be silent and empty. Apart, that is, from the daily drama of a member of staff doing their best to disentangle me from my mother's arms.

'Come on now Steven, I'm sure your mother has things to do at home. She can't stay *here* all morning watching you cry. Besides, don't you want to be with your friends?'

This line of encouragement was *never* going to work. I hated the idea of having *friends*. I just wanted to go home and be with mum. But eventually, the determined member of staff would lead me away— still sobbing—deep into the bowels of the school building.

## 6

## MR WILLIAMS

*I walked around and around in small circles. My hands were clasped firmly over my ears and I hummed a long continuous note to further isolate myself from the world outside my thoughts.*

'*Right then* class, how are we today? Ready for some hard graft?' Mr Williams—teacher, and proud mountain of a rugged Welshman would enquire with intimidating resonance.

'*Right then,* our first lesson will be mathematics. Just follow my instructions, and you won't go wrong.'

In theory, this advice was good, but it would not work for me. I was already anticipating failure and planning my escape.

Mr Williams—complete with humungous ginger sideburns and clashing brown suit—would turn towards the large blackboard behind his desk and begin to write. Immediately his instructions seemed to vaporise into a meaningless verbal fog—pierced only by the excruciating sound of chalk being dragged across a hard black surface.

'Right then, does *everyone* understand?' He'd say without turning to face the rows of identically clad eight-year-olds nodding their heads in the affirmative.

'Right then class, you've got twenty minutes to complete your work.'

Immediately, my classmates sprang into action. Silently calculating on their fingers, and entering the results into their workbooks. I, however, was engrossed *only* in shielding my eyes from the nause-ating intrusion of fluorescent light flickering high above my head.

In desperation I closed my eyes for a few seconds, only to hear a bellowing Mr Williams enquire:

'Tired *Slavin,* are we*?'*

'Shouldn't be tired at *your* age. Early to bed, and up with the lark, that's *my* motto.'

Instantly, the vision of a golden sunrise, a snoring Mr Williams, and a small bird perched on a window ledge was all I could think of. Was Mr Williams *really* woken by a lark each morning? I wondered, as he turned again to his blackboard to scrawl in unintel-ligible screechy white shapes. My heart pounded faster and faster, and I could sense the brooding swell of a major panic attack rising in my gut.

I squinted at the blackboard one final time, and then down at the blank page in my writing pad, knowing that unless a miracle occurred, it was likely to stay that way for ever. The twenty-minute deadline elapsed, and still I had not made a single mark in my workbook. Then, all of a sudden, Mr Williams broke the silence, as if summoning a battalion of Welsh guards to attention:

'*Right then* class, time's up, who's finished?'

Disturbingly… once again, I was the lone straggler in a sea of raised hands. What secret powers did these young super-humans possess? And why was I the *only* one in the class who had not understood a single thing?

Now I could feel the laser like force of Mr Williams' intense gaze. 'Did you not *get-it* Slavin…? Which part *didn't* you understand?' I was confused, he seemed to be offering help, yet his tone was menacing. I had reached breaking point, and before I could say *none of it, sir,* I'd bolted from my seat and out through the classroom door. I ran full-speed along the corridor, passing classrooms on either side where I could see rows of happy, confident children. They were reading, writing and enthusiastically raising their hands in response to their teachers' questions.

Why couldn't I be like them? What was *wrong* with me? And why was I now the only child in the entire school hiding behind the bike shed in the corner of an empty playground?

Sometimes when a member of staff found me hiding behind the bike shed, I would be marched directly into head teacher *Ms Wilkinson's* office. This was an even more terrifying prospect than being sent directly back to class, and meant that I was *really* in trouble.

I'd sit nervously on a squeaky little wooden chair, the one reserved for the *bad* children, until the greying, bespectacled headmistress was ready to acknowledge my presence. This was a wait that would last forever, and one clearly designed to cause the utmost anxiety in any child brought before her.

The other thing I remember about Ms Wilkinson's office was the smell. It was an odious combination of floor polish, stale tobacco, and home made marmalade.

On cold wintry days when it was too wet for outside activities, Ms Wilkinson would invite a handful of favourite pupils into her office to assist in her passion for shredding oranges and cooking them in vats of boiling water. Bag after bag of sugar would be emptied into the steaming metallic pots, as her team of tiny helpers was instructed to: 'STIR FASTER… *FASTER!*'

Once, I too had been among the chosen few—plucked from the crowd and instructed to: 'STIR FASTER, *FASTER…!*' I can, therefore, divulge with accuracy, the innermost secrets of Ms Wilkinson's marmalade manufacturing process.

The morning after a decent downpour of rain, a brand new batch of extra thick orange goo would be left cooling in glass jars stacked neatly in the corner of her office. Each one dated and categorised accordingly.

Whilst waiting on the *naughty* chair I would count the jars, twice over, and then twice over again—attempting to complete the calculation before she began to speak. In my imagination, something *really* terrible would happen, if I were interrupted before the counting finished.

Sometimes I'd become so fixated on counting the jars of marmalade, that when Ms Wilkinson finally looked up at me to speak, I could not immediately respond.

'Steven… *STEVEN.* I'm talking to you.'

'Now… tell me what the problem is *this* time?' She would ask.

A thousand thoughts would rush through my mind —none of them *good.*

Was she angry with me? I couldn't tell. Am I in trouble? Is she going to shout at me? What is going to happen next?

Again, she would ask, '*STEVEN*, ARE YOU LISTENING? What is troubling you this time? Is it something you would like to talk to me about?'

I'd shrug my shoulders and begin to cry. 'I just want to go home, I don't feel well.'

'I shall have to report this to your mother again. She is very worried about your behaviour…'

The confrontation with Ms Wilkinson would end with Mrs Clarke leading me back to class and to the ever-present, ever-shouty Mr Williams.

\* \* \*

For me, school was not about achieving good grades. It was about surviving the harsh overhead lighting and the clattering of furniture on hard shiny floors. It was about the nauseating smell of stale milk escaping from the canteen, and negotiating those long echoing corridors filled with noisy, scampering children.

I'm not sure whether Ms Wilkinson ever fully understood why I was hospitalised and away from school so often. But then, this was the 1960s, and at least thirty years before my brand of developmental disorder was widely recognised.

Unfortunately, the task of obtaining effective autism-friendly education for one's autistic child is a frustrating battle still faced by so many parents. And in these day's of austerity, and cuts to local services, little is likely to change in this regard.

## 7

## BRADLEY DAVIES

The one thing I'd managed to avoid at Preston Park were the bullies. Apart, that is, from the unfortunate incident with Bradley Davies.

Bradley was tall for his age, and, if we're being honest, more than a little plump.

I'm not sure what was troubling Bradley at the time, but for a week or two, his inner demons had turned him into a vicious, leg-kicking thug, with sights set firmly on *me*.

Bradley would pounce on the walk home from school each day, and plant kick after unprovoked kick until he'd turn off into his driveway to greet his adoring mother with the sugary smile of a white-winged angel. A few minutes later I'd arrive home, and mum would ask, 'how did you get those bruises Steven?' I'd shrug my shoulders and say nothing.

Unfortunately, however, for Bradley, his violent

antics were about to come to a painful, and quite unexpected conclusion. On the walk home along College Road one day, Bradley came alongside as usual and aimed hard a kick at the same shinbone he'd targeted the previous day. But this time my reaction was different. Instinctively—and in what felt like slow motion—I felt my right arm swing from well below the waist, and in a long, wide, sweep, land a devastating right hook to the point of his nose.

Bradley fell backwards into Mrs Neville's carefully manicured garden hedge—ripping the skin on his right arm. Suddenly, a drop of dark nose blood appeared on Bradley's grubby white school shirt, then another, and another, with increasing frequency—turning red, his excess of exposed, white belly fat.

Barely breaking my stride, I left Bradley extricating himself from Mrs Neville's thorny foliage, and continued on my journey as if nothing had happened.

I arrived home a few minutes later to find mum waiting for me on the porch. I closed the garden gate and turned to greet her.

'Have a nice day dear?' She enquired, I shrugged my shoulders—something I'd often do when unable to interpret a question.

'What did you do to Bradley Davis?' She said with a puzzled look on her face. Again, I shrugged my shoulders and said nothing.

Mum continued her investigations…

'I've just had his mother on the phone. She says

you clobbered her Bradley and gave him a black eye. I told her *that's* just not possible. My Steven's half the size of your Bradley!'

'She said his school shirt was ruined. I told her I'd have a word with *you* about it.'

Mum gave me a knowing half-smile, and handed me a sandwich and a glass of milk.

Mum never mentioned the incident again. She knew I was the one responsible for adjusting the bones in Bradley's face. But secretly, I bet she was just a tiny bit delighted that her son, had, for once, overcome his fear of people and stood up for himself.

By chance, I bumped into Bradley Davis at a wedding reception a few years ago. I was waiting for him to say, with some amusement:

'Hey Steven, do you remember the punch up we had in 1967?'

But for some reason, he didn't. Had that impressive thump on the nose caused a lasting amnesia? Or was the memory simply too painful to remember?

Either way, I'm happy to report that his nose looked in remarkably good shape. And I don't think my epic right hook was in any way responsible for his shiny bald patch, *or* his ever expanding waist-line.

Oh well, such is life and those inescapable laws of karma...

## 8

# THE ONSET OF OCD

Dressed proudly in Preston Park's team colours, we took our positions on the football field.

I waited nervously on the right wing scanning the opposing team in the pre-match face off. They looked so much bigger and scarier than us. But still, I wasn't about to let size or fear stop me from getting *stuck in*.

The referee's whistle screeched annoyingly in my ear and the epic battle began. For ninety non-stop minutes I chased that heavy, brown ball across a muddy pitch with the speed of a blinkered racehorse, or a crazed, cartoon roadrunner with an out-of-control caffeine rush—rarely looking up to acknowledge my teammates.

But, my abundant, if unregulated enthusiasm had not gone unnoticed by a certain Mr Williams, who, when not intimidating me in class, was in his other role as football coach, yelling instructions at me from the sideline…

'RIGHT THEN SLAVIN, LET'S SEE SOME PASSING. I SAID PASS THE BALL SLAVIN. PASS THE BLASTED BALL. YOU'RE NOT THE ONLY ONE IN THE TEAM Y'KNOW!'

Mr Williams may not have been impressed by my lack of interaction with the other players, but surely he could not fault my determination to win the ball at all costs. Even if this meant putting my life on the line.

On one occasion, I stood bravely on our goal line and made a heroic save by sacrificing the skin on my right thigh to a thunderbolt of a shot by the opposing team's star striker. His name was Kevin, aka Buster. He was twice my size and could strike the ball harder than a mule could kick a barn door.

It was the second half of a crunch match against local rivals *East Lane*. Our goalkeeper was beaten and lying face down in a sea of mud. Only I was positioned to stop Buster from blasting the ball into the back of our net for the third time in as many minutes.

Without hesitation, I threw myself in front of the unstoppable Buster who was hurtling towards our goal area like a demonic steam train. He lifted his boot, and then BANG. His shot was deadly, and it was accurate—driven hard with the weight and power of a cannonball fired in anger. It hit me high up on the thigh, and bounced away from the goal and into the modest crowd of Preston Park supporters who were now chanting, S*LAVIN... SLAVIN*.

I had, single-handedly, preventing Buster from scoring, and when I got home after school I told mum all about what had happened:

'Yes, I know dear,' she replied—glancing at my legs, and the football-shaped patch of dried mud that stung like hell when I later tried to scrape it off.

'We could hear the supporters chanting your name all along Grasmere Avenue from the pitch. We wondered what had happened!'

Of course, we still lost heavily, 4–1 if I remember rightly. But for once, just *once*, I felt like a winner.

At football practice the following day, Mr Williams was back to his usual strict and shouty *self*. Had he forgotten already that I had thwarted Buster? I was a hero, and people had chanted my name. But none of this seemed to impress the stern faced Mr Williams. Instead, he continued to growl undecipherable commands at me from the side of the pitch—his face progressing through every shade of pink to red in unnecessary anger.

'YOU'RE NOT WIDE ENOUGH SLAVIN, GET OUT TO THE RIGHT, PASS IT, *NO NO NO* NOT LIKE THAT. C'MON BOY, GET WIDER. I SAID WIDER SLAVIN, WIDER. WHAT PART OF *WIDER* ARE YOU NOT UNDERSTANDING…?'

Actually, I did not understand *any* of Mr Williams' aggressively delivered tactical suggestions.

What was I supposed to be wider *of*? Just what exactly was an acceptable amount of wide? If only I knew where *wide* was, I could go there, and perhaps he would stop shouting at me.

Soon I was drifting from one, *wrong* position to an apparently even worse, *wrong* position, like a lost sheep trying to find its way home under a hail of verbal bullets.

And then Mr Williams—in his super tight, navy blue track suit, with white *go faster* stripes on the side of each leg—suddenly changed his instructions:

'GET TIGHTER, SLAVIN, I SAID *TIGHTER*… WHAT PART OF *TIGHTER* DO YOU NOT UNDERSTAND…?'

So now he wanted me to get wider and tighter. Is it even possible to be wider *and* tighter of something at the same time? And why did there always have to be some part of *something* I apparently did not understand?

It was all too complicated. I was stressed out and confused, and prayed the earth would open into a great big hole by the centre circle and swallow me up. But of course, it didn't. Instead, I cried, and left the pitch complaining of a stomach ache.

'AHH, DON'T BE SUCH A BABY SLAVIN… YOU'D BETTER GO AND GET CHANGED BACK INTO YOUR UNIFORM,' he sneered as I limped off the pitch, doubled over in pain from my groaning gut.

Could it be that Mr Williams had been partially

responsible for the onset of my *Obsessive Compulsive Disorder* at the tender age of eight? This would explain why my earliest experiences of the condition occurred on the football field.

From nowhere, I developed the compulsion to take an even number of steps before I could cross any of the white lines marked on the pitch.

Four steps seemed to be the best number, but two would suffice if I was in a hurry. *Two* sets of two was okay, but *three* sets of two was not. Having a number *three* in the equation would—at least in my imagination—mean that something *really* bad may happen as a result.

Adhering to all of these rules was exhausting. Running across a football pitch now required a complex set of calculations, balletic footwork, and quick decision making. Should I attempt to cross the halfway line by taking four small strides? Or risk falling flat on my face by taking two *really* big ones?

And soon my counting rituals spread to other areas of life. Each day, a new compulsion arrived to imprison me like the unhappy servant to an unforgiving subconscious mind.

I remember how my compulsive need to count, and swallow an *even* number of times made the simple task of walking along the pavement so extraordinarily difficult.

At times I was unable to take a single step without counting to two, four or eight whilst swallowing an equal amount of times. This often produced the strange spectacle of having one leg suspended in mid-air, until I could summon up another set of two swallows. Then I could safely touch down without something terrible happening to me or mum. This was especially difficult in hot weather when my throat was dry, and saliva was in short supply.

Other times, I'd attempt to swallow eight times before entering a room. Or I'd need to touch an object with both hands until it *felt* okay—until I could feel a perfect synchronicity of pressure on both hands.

The neighbours would simply shrug their shoulders when they saw me coming along and think, 'here comes that strange Slavin boy again, he's not *right* you know…'

Historically, there have been differing opinions among psychologists as to whether OCD and autism can co-exist. In my opinion there is little doubt that these conditions can, and often do. After all, OCD is an anxiety driven condition, and what do people on the autism spectrum struggle with more than anything? Yes, it's anxiety.

Also, there are misconceptions about the obsessive-repetitive trait's seen in autism, and the compulsive needs of OCD sufferers. But there *are* subtle differences.

It's been said that autistic people find comfort in routine and ritualisation. It gives them a degree of control over a world they find confusing.

Conversely, OCD is a mental health disorder in which the sufferer feels that harm may befall them or a loved one, if their compulsions are not adhered to. Please note: This is a very brief description of OCD.

There is, at present, a very real problem faced by doctors—recognising and then treating OCD in people with autism. To date, I have not come across a single mental health professional, with sufficient knowledge of autism, capable of adjusting traditionally applied OCD treatments so they will work for those of us on the autistic spectrum.

OCD remains an incurable constant in my life. Talking therapies such as Cognitive Behavioural Therapy have not worked for me, but a daily dose of *Sertraline* has—but only a little. My view is simple and pragmatic: Whatever helps me get through the day, helps me get through the day. As long as it's legal, I'm in. And if it means adding substantially to the profits of those *evil* pharmaceutical companies, then so be it, life is just too short to worry about such things.

## 9

# GRASMERE AVENUE

On sunny Sunday afternoons, Grasmere Avenue felt like the safest place on earth. Little had changed in that perfect picture of suburbia since the houses grew from green fields and farmland in the early 1930s.

From up and down our tree-lined avenue would come the intoxicating aroma of freshly mowed lawns, and the reassuring sound of hedge cutters clicking away like distant Woodpeckers in the warm, and otherwise silent air.

Through my first floor bedroom window at the front of the house, my bird's-eye view was serene. Rows of pleasant gardens stretched out on either side of ours. Each one separated into identikit squares of perfect grass, flower-filled borders and the occasional plastic-gnome.

Opposite, I could see the green, spiky outline of a Monkey Puzzle tree. When covered in snow, its branches became white and frozen like some curious misshapen Christmas tree. And in warmer months, the sun would set behind it in orange and purple layers, to cast a long, spidery shadow across the pavement and onto the road.

Turning to view my modestly sized bedroom, I'd see walls lined with football posters, and pictures of magnificent steam locomotives with names like *The Flying Scotsman* and *The Cheltenham Flyer*.

Above my bed, bookshelves strained under the weight of thrillers, atlases and golfing tuitionals.

Once, a shelf gave way causing an entire collection of the *Adventures of Biggles*, and all four volumes of *History of The English Speaking Peoples* by *Churchill* to tumble mercilessly onto the bridge of my nose. Fortunately, the only permanent casualty of this painful literary avalanche was a blood-spattered volume of *Biggles*. The one in which our wartime hero lands his *Sopwith Camel* behind enemy lines to destroy a German ammunition dump —before returning home across the channel in time to see the sun rise over Dover's gleaming white cliffs.

*Note to Reader*: If you are under forty years of age, or generally confused about what I've just described—can I suggest *Google*. Or better still, buy a copy of Biggles. The one where he lands behind enemy lines and ...

If the fictional *Biggles* was imbued with copious

amounts of good old British, bulldog spirit, then so was the very real *Charles White* next door.

*Mr* White, as we knew him for almost half a century, had a well paid job in the city. Each morning he'd set off to work along Grasmere Avenue—splendid in black pinstripes, a briefcase in one hand, and a neatly folded copy of *The Times* in the other.

This would leave *Gwen White*—or *Mrs* White, as we knew *her* for almost half a century—to cook, clean and gossip until Mr White re-appeared at precisely 6:30 pm.

On Sundays, Mr White could be found toiling away in the garden under the hot, midday sun. The sleeves of his favourite gardening shirt would be rolled up high to reveal hairy forearms—damp with honest perspiration. Deeper pools of sweat would leak from the edge of his receding hairline as he mowed back and forth till 3 pm, when he'd stop to take afternoon tea, and catch up with the latest cricket scores on the BBC.

With 3 pm formalities fulfilled, gardening would resume amidst genteel mutterings on the poor state of his beloved game.

Occasionally, Mr White would catch me peering at him through a gap in the adjoining slatted-wood fence. He'd attempt to engage me in conversation about either—*the cricket*, *the football*, or, *the weather*. Sometimes, all three topics would be rolled into one long sentence that didn't appear to require a response, so I didn't always give one…

'Shame about all this rain we've been having lately,' he'd say—looking as though he was about to keel over with heatstroke. 'Been playing havoc with the cricket… Still, I expect Sweden would have beaten us in the football the other night, regardless of the weather. Oh well, better get this lawn finished before it rains…'

I'd look up into the clearest of cloud free, deep blue summer skies and wonder what the hell he was talking about. Perhaps this was Mr White *doing* what my speech therapist called *small talk*. After all, we hadn't seen rain in weeks, and more importantly, mum hadn't reported any aching bones to confirm Mr White's absurd suspicion of a pending downpour.

*Mrs* White, on the other hand, was not so affable. I could not understand her body language at all. Was she being rude, or shy, or that *other* thing mum often called her—*anti-Semitic*? Usually, mum abbreviated this to just *anti.* She hated confrontation and thought it was generally safer to call someone *anti…* and leave off the *Semitic* bit—just in case.

Mrs White rarely spoke to me or mum over the garden fence. She'd prefer to pluck her drying prewar underwear from the washing line as quickly as she could, then scamper back inside the house to avoid making conversation.

'What's up with that silly cow *this* time?' Mum would say—shaking her head in disgust…

'People think we're dirty Jews *Steven*, that's why they won't talk to us—the English have *their* ways of doing things, and we have ours.'

I remember thinking: but if we're not *English*, how come I got so angry and upset when we were beaten 1-0 by Sweden in the football the other night? Didn't my display of blind, unhinged, patriotism account for *anything…?*

# 10

## GRANDPA

In 1967, Grasmere Avenue was almost completely free of noisy, passing traffic. Apart, that is, from the familiar roar of a *Ford's* tiny engine being revved to the point of explosion quickly, followed by a thunderous crunching of gears.

From previous experience, mum and I knew the disturbing mechanical symphony would not be over until we'd hear that teeth-clenching grind of metal hubcaps against a hard, concrete curb. A moment of silence would follow, and then the short, sharp toot of an unimpressive car horn—just to let us know he'd arrived.

This was the unmistakable sound of grandpa dropping by for a salt beef sandwich and an afternoon nap.

It was easy to spot grandpa's car. It would be the one parked with three wheels on the road and one on the pavement. Or sometimes two wheels on the road and *two* on the pavement, but never with all four wheels *on* the tarmac at the same time, and in perfect alignment with the attractive grass verge running the entire length of Grasmere Avenue.

Grandpa was not good at parking, or, in fact, driving, *or*, for that matter, reading road signs that said important things like:

- *NO ENTRY!*

- *STOP!*

- *ROADWORKS AHEAD–PLEASE DRIVE SLOWLY!*

It wasn't that he didn't care about road safety. It's just that, well… detail wasn't really grandpa's *thing*.

Mum and I would stand by the front door to greet the tall, elegantly dressed man as he'd walk straight past us with just a short, '*alright*?' And then he'd plonk himself down in his favourite armchair to read the newspaper and snooze.

But whatever Grandpa may have lacked in social graces, he more than made up for in style. In thirty years, I cannot recall seeing him even once, without perfectly pressed grey trousers, a silk cravat and a tweed flat cap.

Grandpa emitted just the slightest whiff of a lovable Cockney rogue. Not, I hasten to add, of the criminal or gangland variety; more of someone that had learned through the school of hard knocks that sometimes, it was necessary to bend the rules—*just* a little bit.

I loved grandpa and always looked forward to seeing him, but, as he sat at the head of the Friday night *Shabbat* table, the vacant seats either side of his would serve as a stark reminder to all who dared to dine, that grandpa was about to devour a bowl of mum's homemade chicken soup.

Tentatively, mum would place the piping hot soup in front of him, and then immediately dive for cover before he could take his first mighty slurp. Then, as if the hot flavoursome broth had been caught in the violent upward thrust of a tornado vortex, grandpa's soup would lift from his bowl and into his mouth somehow bypassing his spoon on the way.

Dining with my oblivious grandpa was not unlike observing a mighty water pump emptying the Red Sea dry with a single, long, loud *suck*. After this, he would retire back to his comfortable armchair and fall asleep until it was time to leave.

Apart from mealtimes, the only occasions I *didn't* feel entirely comfortable with grandpa, was as a passenger in the front seat of his beloved canary-yellow *Ford Anglia*.

No one could complain about its immaculately kept interior and pleasant smell of freshly squeezed lemons—from a freshly squeezed can of lemon furniture polish. But it was impossible to ignore the fact that you were probably strapping yourself into the cleanest, sweetest smelling deathtrap known to man.

Reaching across to insert my seat belt into its sparkling chrome receptacle, I'd think, *I hope I'll get to see mum again.* And then, with a sudden lurch forward, or sometimes backwards, we were *off*—on a literal spin around the block, whilst mum brewed the tea and sliced some honey cake—just in case grandpa and I made it back alive, and could stomach some light refreshments without throwing up.

Mum said her father's driving was, 'extremely dangerous on a good day, and very likely to kill someone on a bad one.' A sentiment whole heartedly endorsed by dad.

Grandpa had, in fact, been terrorising the king's highway in one of those new-fangled automobile things from the moment peace broke out in 1945. And in those early Wild West days of motoring, it was simply a case of: Hit the gas, and hope for the best —precisely what grandpa continued to do until somewhere around 1984.

By the time grandpa *Larry*—real name *Isaac*—had retired from driving, he'd *written-off* not only his canary-yellow Ford Anglia, but also a blue and white Ford Anglia, and a Ford Cortina that had, apparently, once been white, but due to a case of terminal rust, ended its days as a sort of orangy-bronze. He'd also partially demolished his brick built garage whilst reversing into it—*literally* reversing into it.

But the day grandpa lost control on that busy round-a-bout on the Kingsbury Road and ended up two-feet off the ground, wedged between a concrete post and the glass shopfront of a BMW showroom, was the day he finally conceded that, well, perhaps driving *wasn't* for him anymore. The motorists of North West London rejoiced, and mum sighed in relief, knowing that from now on grandpa would be letting the train take the *strain.*

Apart from mum, grandpa was the only person I could be alone with without getting upset or a *really* bad stomach ache. He was kind and made me laugh a lot. I adored his amusing impressions of *Hitler* and *Stalin,* and other disagreeable historical figures that had caused such darkness to befall the people of his generation.

He'd describe how the Cossacks had ridden into his parent's town on horseback, and expelled all the Jews in the 1904 pogroms—and about their arrival, penniless and unwanted in England.

Grandpa would say:

'We lived in Code Street, Whitechapel, near

where Jack the Ripper killed all of those women. Five of us lived in two rooms above the stable where we kept the horse.'

'That horse had more space that *we* did,' he'd add, to make me laugh at the absurd notion.

Grandpa told me about the 1936 *Battle of Cable Street* when *Oswald Mosley's* army of black shirted fascists marched through the neighbourhood, seeking to rid the East End of its Jewish population—only to be thwarted by workers from the nearby docks confronting them with fists and iron bars.

Grandpa's vocabulary was peppered with *Yiddish* and a dash of *Hebrew*. *Geyn Pishn,* for example, meant that he needed to use the bathroom. And when he called me *Boychik*—as indeed, he often did— grandpa was definitely *not* comparing me to a Thai sex worker of uncertain gender. *Boychik* is simply a Yiddish term of endearment that suffers from a rather unfortunate coincidence.

When Grandpa passed away, he left us with a cheeky smile on his face. And whenever I think of him, an affectionate smile appears on mine.

The nurses at the hospital where he spent his final days told mum that one minute he was laughing and joking with them—probably telling them how in the 1920s he'd jumped ship in New York and wound up Canada, or the West Indies and then… quite suddenly, he was *gone*.

Sometimes I get the distinct feeling that grandpa

is near me somehow—still a vision of cockney style, and with that familiar cheeky grin. But I know that as long as he's *up there* somewhere, keeping watch, everything will *always* be okay in the end.

God bless you grandpa. I'll see you again one day.

## 11

## A TEAM
## OF ONE

*Some people on the autistic spectrum seek the company of others but lack the necessary social skills to sustain friendships.*

*I, however, simply prefer to be alone.*

During the holidays and on weekends when the other children my age were kicking footballs around the local park with friends, I was busy devising all sorts of ingenious methods for playing team sports *alone*, and from within the safe confines of home.

To this end, the concrete wall at the bottom of the garden became my inanimate and unfaltering friend.

Through rain and shine, and with unquestioning reliability, that wall rebounded the ball back to me with the minimum of fuss and zero conversation. Whether it was football, tennis, cricket or golf, my concrete friend was *there* for me.

It was back-stop, target, and boundary—a safe place to climb, and a sturdy support for handstand practice.

During the summer months, its warm textured surface doubled as a calming sensory place on which I could rest the palms of my hands, and the side of my face.

And when January brought it's freezing fog, and temperatures that seemed to plummet well below the winters we have now. I'd wake to the aftermath of an overnight blizzard, and wonder at the miraculous transformation of my little sporting arena into a quiet sea of fresh white snow.

Meanwhile, my *wall* waited silently for me to put on my warm coat and wellies, and rush out to aim a snowball or two.

I simply loved the way snow changed *everything*. In fact, I yearned for *any* kind of dramatic event that meant I could avoid school for a while: Storms, doctor's orders, a death in the family. It wouldn't matter. As long as I could stay at home for a few days with mum and play in the back garden.

Mum would say:

'Don't stay out there for too long *Steven*— remember you haven't been well lately.'

*'You haven't been well lately,'* was mum's way of reminding me that I was supposed to be recuperating with as little stress as possible after yet another lengthy stay in the psych ward at Great Ormond

Street Hospital. But I was mot deterred. And when spring arrived to melt the snow, my garden would become something akin to *Wembley Stadium*. I'd exit through the kitchen door and out onto the hallowed turf to take my place alongside the era's footballing greats—*George Best, Bobby Charlton* and *Pele*—for another exciting day of *solo*, team sport.

I'd often catch Mrs White—our elusive next door neighbour—peering covertly from her first floor bedroom window. I'd not see her face, but would know she was there by the way her floral curtains would carefully shift into gaps through which my *odd* behaviour could be analysed in the garden below.

I could just imagine her thinking—*why is that peculiar child hugging the wall again?* And she would have also wondered about my non-stop dialogue with a garden full of invisible *friends*.

She would hear…

'Slavin, the brilliant centre-forward for Chelsea has the ball. He goes past one defender, he goes past two, the Manchester United goal is in sight, the crowd roars with excitement, he goes to shoot… OH NO! He's been brought down by Bobby Charlton. What a dirty foul! The Chelsea fans are incensed. This could be a penalty… YES… the referee's *given* it. The tense crowd quietens to a hush. Slavin approaches the ball… he *hits* it. BANG! YES, it's in the back of the net. What a hero!' The crowd screams. They are elated. Charlton crouches—holding his head in shame…'

'One more tackle like that *Charlton*, and your off! Warns the ref.'

Yes, as well as being all eleven players on *my* team, I was also, eleven members of the opposing team, the referee, the commentator, and a thirty-thousand-strong crowd of impassioned fans willing me on to greater heroic deeds. And with a garden so full of invisible, world-class sportsmen I had no need for *real* people. My imaginary friends would simply disappear as soon as I stopped thinking about them—perfect really.

All was not perfect, however, in the opinion of my psychiatrist. He, along with my parents, were growing increasingly concerned about my self-imposed social isolation. During my final year of primary school, I was rarely able to leave the house without collapsing into uncontrollable floods of tears, or bent double with searing stomach pain.

If another six week hospital admission couldn't *fix* me in time to start *big* school in September 1970, then I would be sent away to, '*an institution for maladjusted boys.*'

The choice was stark. And the consequence of *not* achieving an impossible cure by the end of summer only added to the heavy weight of anxiety that was making me ill in the first place.

## 12

## A NEW DECADE

*The box over there in the corner, the one labelled: Not Quite Right. That's Steven's box. He likes it over there, away from all the other boxes labelled Normal.*

It was July 1970 and the colourful idealism of the previous decade's short, heady dream was sliding into the harsh black and white reality of economic gloom.

Yet, still, the young pedestrians of London continued to adorn the best of 60s fashion as though they were out-of-date clothes horses in search of new lands to graze.

And as mum and I made our way from Russell Square Tube Station to Great Ormond Street Hospital, we'd weave in and out of short-haired girls in *Mary Quant* inspired miniskirts, and long-haired men in purple, crushed velvet bell-bottoms—partially hidden beneath long Afghan coats.

Bizarrely, mum and I once found ourselves shopping alongside London's elite fashionistas in, of all places, that bastion of 60s style—*BIBA*.

I cannot begin to imagine why mum thought this was the best place to buy my new pyjamas for my upcoming hospital admission that summer. Why deviate from the usual *Woolworths* or *Marks & Spencer?* I thought.

Did she really think I'd feel comfortable being the only child in the psych ward wearing black and gold pure silk nightwear? Perhaps mum just wanted to catch a brief glimpse of how the *other half* lived—the *other half* that could afford to buy such things in BIBA.

Our shopping trip to BIBA, however, did not go as planned. After just a few minutes of pyjama hunting, mum and I were startled by the sound of a fire alarm. Hundreds of trendy young shoppers were fleeing towards the exit sign, and out onto an equally upmarket Kensington High Street.

The reason for their swift evacuation, and the end to our high-end retail experience was a *plausible* bomb threat by the *Irish Republican Army*. Or, at least that's what the woman announced over the loudspeaker system.

In that delightfully measured tone favoured by the

BBC when delivering the nightly shipping forecast, it was calmly announced that:

*'We have been informed there may be a bomb in this store. Kindly make your way to the exit in an orderly fashion. Thank you for shopping at BIBA!'*

On TV later that day, the news reporter said it had, in fact, been nothing more than a cruel hoax designed to cause chaos rather than injury. But in the light of the ongoing bombing campaign in which so many people had been killed, mum and I were happy with our decision to suspend shopping activities for the afternoon, and return home to the relative safety of Grasmere Avenue. Albeit, without my sexy new silk pyjamas.

## 13

### HOSPITAL: 1970

*'Steven is currently in hospital awaiting placement in a school for maladjusted boys…'*
*—Great Ormond Street Hospital Summer 1970.*

The only *good* thing about being in hospital that summer, was that I had permission to stay up later than usual to watch the Mexico World Cup football in the visitors waiting room.

I remember being glued to the black, white and grey images of a mighty *Brazil,* and how they ran footballing rings around any team daring to confront them. And the England team—initially, still aglow from their World Cup triumph four years earlier— had, somewhat predictably, reverted to their usual faltering averageness. A fate endured by frustrated supporters ever since twelfth-century peasants first kicked a stuffed sheep's bladder from one village to the next.

The only *other* thing that broke the monotony of those long, hazy hospital days, were the afternoon visits from mum. She'd arrive with a bag of goodies, looking tired and stressed.

Mum must have dreaded those visits. My reliance on her as my sole interface with the world put her directly in the firing line for my inevitable barrage of unanswerable questions:

'How long will I be in here for? What is the name of my new doctor? What happens if I can't sleep? When can I go home?'

It was always: *'When can I go home?'*

The answers were always the same, but then, *so* were the questions…

'I've told you already *Steven*, the doctors don't know what's wrong with you. They want to find out why you won't go to school, and why you get so upset over everything.'

Mum was right. The doctors *were* baffled. I was a mystery condition without a cure—a medical curiosity, and of great interest to my inquisitive team of men in white coats.

Apart from the occasional treat of staying up late to watch the World Cup football, my routine was as unchanging as England's inability to impress on the pitch:

- •Breakfast at 7:30
- •Lunch at 12:30
- •Dinner at 6
- •Bath at 7
- •Medication at 7:30
- •Bed at 8

The 7 *am* slot was reserved for my morning medication. I'd open my blurry eyes to the sight of a nurse standing over me with a small plastic container. Inside were my special *happy-day-time-pills*.

'Time to wake up now Steven, and how do we feel today?' The nurse would ask. But I could not answer. After a night of heavy, drug induced sleep, I'd awake feeling utterly wiped out, and quite unable to string a sentence together.

Then, by mid-morning my 7 am chemical cosh would begin to take effect, and stagnate my thoughts in a *different* way until 7:30 pm—when it was time for my *magic-sleepy-time*-pills.

And so, the endless rotation of medication and therapy continued day after muddled day, until I'd lost all track of time.

Sometimes the nurse would take me along to Dr Howarth's office for a *chat*. He was a gentle, well-spoken man in his mid-thirties. One of a new breed of psychiatrists familiar with the latest research into childhood mental disorder.

'Tell me about the pictures you drew in art therapy,' he'd ask.

'Why do you suppose they're so full of dark clouds?'

I'd say nothing and shrug my shoulders.

'Why do you find it so difficult to make eye contact with me *Steven*?' He'd continue.

'If I tell you, can I go home?' I'd reply in hopeless negotiation.

'I feel better now, I promise not to cry any more, and I'll go to school?'

Dr Howarth would smile kindly and say, 'I think it's best you stay here for a while, so we can find out what the problem is and make you better…'


August 1970

With the summer of 1970 coming to an end, I knew that at some point the thorny subject of my education would need to be addressed. I couldn't stay in hospital for ever, and my preferred option of staying home with mum was obviously out of the question.

I also knew that soon, the kids from Preston Park Primary would dress in their brand new secondary school uniforms—ready to cross the uneasy bridge to adolescence in a way that I could not.

And so I was not particularly surprised when Dr Howarth sat on the end of my hospital bed one afternoon and announced his plans for my future…

'We don't think you'll be able cope at *normal* school Steven, so we've decided to send you away to a special type of boarding school in Dorset. It's called *Monkton Wyld,* and you'll be starting there in a few weeks time. The funding is in place, and my decision is final…'

## 14

---

# MONKTON WYLD

Autumn 1970: Age Eleven

The big scary day had arrived.

With my suitcase in the back of dad's trusty old *Austin*, and mum sitting nervously on the front passenger seat, we set off on the long journey to the faraway land of West Dorset. And in 1970, the drive to Monkton Wyld really *did* feel like a challenging adventure to a previously unexplored world. Back then there *were* no motorways en route, or cars capable of cruising indefinitely at seventy-miles per-hour. Dad's car struggled to maintain speeds greater than *thirty* for any length of time. Even the slightest hint of an incline was likely to push the Austin's tiny engine to the edge of its unimpressive limits.

For what felt like an eternity, we followed the rise and fall of undulating black tarmac. The urban sprawl giving way to the farms and woodland connecting *Basingstoke* to Salisbury, *Middle Wallop* to *Blandford Forum, Whitchurch Canonicorum to Marshwood,* and finally on to *Monkton Wyld.*

Some five-hours later, dad turned off the main coastal road, and down into a single track lane so steep, it felt as though we were driving off the edge of the world.

We continued to descend at a snail's pace, hoping a vehicle would not approach from the opposite direction and force dad to reverse backwards to the top of the winding lane, as though trapped inside a gigantic game of snakes and ladders.

Deeper and deeper we drove down into the mouth of the valley's steep decline. Above us, the sky disappearing and reappearing repeatedly through the overhang of thick green foliage—only to be swallowed again and again by towering, claustrophobic hedgerows closing in on either side.

Finally, a sign appeared for Monkton Wyld. We turned off into a dark, tree-lined driveway that crunched and bumped under our struggling tyres.

We had arrived.

Feeling sick from the gut-wrenching stench of burnt petrol fumes, I climbed out of dad's surprisingly robust little *Austin,* and looked up in horror at the hellish grey building rising high above me into a rain-ready sky.

Surely *this* can't be it, I thought—pinching myself

to see if I had woken into some godawful nightmare. Everywhere, horrific stone gargoyles peeked out from moss-stained corners, and even the name—*Monkton Wyld,* sounded to me like a Victorian lunatic asylum that would become a prime location for *Dracula* movies, and *Devil Worship for Dummies* seminars on alternate weekends.

I fully expected to see, within those walls: Padded cells and straitjackets, barred windows and restraining chains. This was an institution capable of inflicting unimaginable cruelty to any child who dared to enter. A place from which there could be no escape. Surely, I would never see mum, or the comforts of our safe suburban home ever again.

Suddenly, I heard the doors of dad's little Austin slam shut. And then with a puff of smoke from it's rusting exhaust-pipe, he manoeuvred carefully towards the end of the driveway, and disappeared into the lane. And then there was silence. I was alone… I'd never been so alone. I wanted to run after dad's car and shout, 'don't leave me here, I promise I'll be good and go to *normal* school!' But it was too late. Soon the Austin would be trundling along the coastal road in the hope of making it back to London in one piece.

'Come on Steven, let's go up to your room and get you unpacked,' said a kindly member of staff. 'You'll be fine here once you get used to it. Besides, it's only six weeks till the half-term break, and you'll see your parents again...'

Monkton Wyld School is, in fact, an early Victorian rectory built in the Gothic style by a wealthy family in 1848. Its fourteen acres of field and woodland populate the slopes of a steep green valley, rising high above the roof of the old house on all sides. The entrance is an imposing castle-like, wooden door—arch shaped, and fortified by a dozen sturdy rivets. Once inside, the musky whiff of antiquity over-whelms, and clings to every breath of damp Victorian air made cold by deep sandstone walls.

For the eleven-year-old *me*, it was easy to believe that something terrifying must lurk around every strange and shadowy corner. Yet, despite the many accounts of other-worldly encounters, I did not expe-rience my first apparition until 1974, when...

In the half-light of a gloomy autumn afternoon, I witnessed the ghostly figure of an old woman follow my unaware friend *Tom,* along the top floor corridor of the old house, and into his bedroom. The floating grey-brown apparition was of a nineteenth-century woman in her latter years. She wore a full-length, high-collared, bustled dress, and on the end of her nose, perched a small pair of spectacles—no doubt ready to allow a stern gaze upon any unruly Victorian child in her care.

Yet, surprisingly, I felt no fear during my encounter with the curious visitor from another time. After all, this was *her* home as well as mine. Even if it *was* one we shared in different dimensions!

An extra layer of strangeness was added to this memory, when, at a school reunion in 2014, I raised the subject of my ghostly experience with another ex-pupil.

'Oh, you mean *The Grey Lady,*' he exclaimed—surprised that I'd not heard her described in this way before.

'Yes,' he continued,

'Loads of us saw her float along the top floor of the old house in the 1960s. It's the ghost of someone called *Beale.* She's buried in the Victorian churchyard across the road from the school…'

I declined his offer of a sightseeing trip to visit the grave of *Beale,* on the grounds that some things are better left alone. Anyhow, it was getting dark, and I really didn't want to risk initialising any further visitations.

That night, I slept with the light on—*just in case!*

Monkton Wyld was, and still is, a building devoid of frills or unnecessary refinement—austere, and virtually unchanged since its construction. None of the bedrooms in the main house were equipped with heating, and only lukewarm water would flow disappointingly from the hot tap when washing on ice-cold winter mornings.

Occasionally, a thick sea-mist would roll in from the nearby Jurassic coast to turn the deep surrounding valley into a ghostly white lake—a cold swirling entity into which the old house may disappear for days on end.

Yet, even in 2018, I remain utterly captivated by the magic of Monkton Wyld. It is, indeed, a place I shall never truly leave.

## Early Days at Monkton

My first few weeks as a Monkton Wylder, however, were neither magical *or* wondrous. In fact, I was utterly crippled by home-sickness, and desperately wanted to see mum.

A former teacher at the school—now in his nineties—reminded me at a recent reunion that I was, 'too depressed to even get out of bed that first week.'

But once resigned to the *cruel* reality of my new circumstances, I tentatively made my way down the steep rickety staircase to join the hustle and bustle of Monkton's alien society. This uneasy peace could not, however, dissuade me from hatching a succession of ingenious escape plans…

In the dead of night, and dressed only in my stripy pyjamas, I climbed out of my bedroom window on the first floor, and down the Wisteria that clung to the flint fascia of the exterior wall. But as I lowered myself down onto the cold tarmac, I was greeted by a member of staff who calmly led me back inside the building and upstairs to my room without saying a word.

On reflection, being caught was probably a *good* thing. Stage *two* of my escape plan would have meant a moonlit trek along a dangerous woodland path, and a four mile walk to Axminster. Here I would board the London train with neither a ticket, *or* a penny to my name. Another factor I hadn't considered, was the small matter of arriving in Central London some five hours later, still dressed only in my stripy pyjamas. How would I have ever found my way home across the city to mum's house in the suburbs?

If ever a plan was destined to end badly, it was *this* one.

Escape Attempt number Two: One afternoon, I simply took off along the lane, *again*, towards the small market town of Axminster—famed for its manufacture of fine carpet, and excellent rail links to London-Waterloo. But this time, my escape was thwarted by a member of staff returning at some speed in the school's green Land Rover.

The vehicle screeched to a halt, and an irritated English teacher jumped out…

'Where do you think *you're* going? You should not be out here on your own!' He announced angrily.

We drove back to school, and again, nothing further was said about the incident.

It was like one of those horror movies when someone tries in vain to escape his evil captors, only to find that all roads lead back to their place of imprisonment.

Gradually, however, as the weeks went by and my homesickness decreased, I began to enjoy the activities on offer at Monkton. There was: Football, pottery, horse riding, cricket, archery, hockey, canoeing, yoga and all sorts of interesting things to do. And whilst the risk of an emotional meltdown was never far away, the breakdowns became fewer, and my self-confidence greater.

At Monkton Wyld, I had the freedom to wander off into the quiet countryside whenever I needed to be alone, or to chat with some of the older pupils who had kindly taken me under their collective wing, if I was worried about anything.

Monkton's informal style of education, and easy-going culture allowed me to break my unhealthy dependence on mum. I was *forced* to think for myself, and to become self-reliant. Dr Howarth's decision to send me away to boarding school had turned out to be a good one. And so, aided by my daily intake of mood stabilisers and tranquillisers, I eventually became a proud member of the Monkton Wyld *family*.

On average, Monkton Wyld's eclectic population of eleven to seventeen-year-olds numbered fifty-eight at any one time. Some were long-haired, afghan coat wearing boys, and others were barefoot girls in skimpy cheesecloth blouses that left little to the imagination of an impressionable eleven-year-old boy.

Also present, but far less common were the strait-laced, aristocratic types with short hair and accents suitable for the dining tables of Buckingham Palace. This rare species of Monkton Wylder could be found clustered together in quiet corners of the Old Library—playing chess and studying Latin. Occasionally, the studious ones would emerge to refill their teacups with milky Earl Grey, pausing between sips to discuss the finer points of *Homers Odyssey,* or *Iliad.*

At various times Monkton was also home for children of American academics, the English aristocracy, famous musicians, and of *The Beatles* inner sanctum, the odd Hollywood A-lister, and—after I'd left—even an Arab Prince or two.

The idea was, that, somehow by osmosis, the supposedly well-adjusted kids would help the emotionally disturbed ones like me become more functional. Or at least that's how it was explained to me at the time. Whilst this lofty goal may have seemed good in principle, I'm not sure how well the concept worked in practice. I can think of a number of *well-adjusted* twelve-year-old pupils for whom the lure of drugs and alcohol led them, eventually, to become decidedly less functional than I.

Monkton practised a style of education known as *Progressive.*

Apart from a few compulsory lessons, we could attend *any* lesson in *any* classroom at *any* time. This type of person-centred education worked especially well for the developmentally challenged kids that could not learn at the same pace as their peers. It did, however, mean that class sizes and age ranges were unpredictable. For example, an eleven-year-old on the first page of *Science for Beginners* may share a classroom with a seventeen-year-old studying advanced physics, whilst a group of giggling thirteen-year-olds experimented in the chemistry area by turning cow excrement, collected from the field, into highly flammable methane gas. Hilarious indeed, yet surprisingly dangerous.

Sometimes the decision on which class to attend was based on one of *two* factors—the popularity of the teacher, and the *weather.* Yes, the weather...

During the dark Dorset winters, my academic achievements were largely determined by the height of the snow piled up against Monkton's Gothic exterior, and by the thickness of the ice clinging to the *inside* of the classroom windows.

When the temperature dropped below zero, the English and History rooms—known for being the warmest—were packed full of denim-clad pupils basking in the bright orange glow of a blazing coal fire. Suddenly my passion for Shakespeare, and the

Ancient Greeks would reach levels of enthusiasm not possible in June.

During the summer months, we could abandon the classrooms altogether in favour of the grassy terraces. Here, under a vast blue sky, we lay out our books and stationary, amongst the sweet-smelling wild flowers —disturbed only by the gentle hum of overweight bumblebees labouring in the morning heat.

Regardless of the weather, lessons would end at lunchtime, and in the afternoon's we'd participate in a range of arts, crafts and sports.

At around 6 pm, most of the staff would disappear to their homes in local villages, leaving just two members of staff—one male, and one female—to watch over the entire school until the following morning. This was when all the *good* stuff happened.

Notable amongst these fun extra-curricular activities were the illicit parties in the woods, and frequent trips to Axcotte—the local cider farm, to stock up on refreshments.

The journey to, and from Axcotte was a challenging, five-mile walk along quiet country lanes. But for the more adventurous, a good half-a-mile could be saved by cutting through the fields and along the treacherous *Blacksnake*—a little known path that would emerge onto a dirt road close to Axcotte's main entrance.

Then there was the customary routine of lowering one's voice, puffing out one's chest, and stretching one's frame to achieve the maximum height and width. This was usually all it took to convince the cider farm's owner that, 'although we may only look *twelve*, we were, in fact, immature *eighteen-year-olds*, and therefore legally entitled to buy alcohol.'

And so, we'd stagger back to school burdened by backpacks loaded with gallon containers of swishing orange liquid—the essential ingredient for an evening of drunken entertainment in the woods.

But it was after midnight when the *truly* audacious would leave their bedrooms to brave the darkened corridors of the old house, and cross the cobblestone courtyard to the room of a girl, or boy friend.

For other *midnight-walkers,* the nocturnal mission was simply for the thrill of encountering something supernatural in that eerie gothic space. Usually, however, the only surprise would be a squeaky floorboard—which at 2:30 am was louder than a mighty Oak falling in the forest on a quiet night.

These unfortunate adventurers in stripy nightwear would be sent back to bed by an angry overnight teacher, warning, 'do *not* let me catch you midnight-walking again…!'

Usually, a lacklustre lashing from a tired teacher's tongue would be the only punishment for those caught hiding in the shadows after midnight when they should have been safely tucked up in bed.

Quite frankly, getting oneself expelled from

Monkton Wyld was not an easy task. I once bought an air rifle and five-hundred lead pellets from a friend who'd smuggled it into school at the beginning of term.

In all, the deal set me back £5.50 in hard cash and a *Jethro Tull* album—a bargain for such a fine piece of near-lethal machinery.

When I wasn't firing shots into the home-made target hanging on my bedroom wall, the air rifle was kept hidden under a loose floorboard next to my bed. One day, however, *Glynis*, the nosey cleaning lady found it, and promptly handed it over to a member of staff for confiscation.

Nowadays, this incident would probably trigger a swift visit by a crack squad of armed police. Military helicopters would circle overhead, and sensational breaking news reports would repeat endlessly on the nation's TV screens—*GUN FOUND AT SCHOOL FOR MENTALLY DISTURBED CHILDREN...!*

The funny thing was, at no time was I ever reprimanded or warned in no uncertain terms that if I was ever found with firearms *again,* I'd be sent home in disgrace.

Shortly after the air rifle incident, I bought a deadly steel catapult from Mark *bendy* Jackson.

Jackson was a slightly odd character who never said much. His bedroom was opposite mine, and he'd spend most of his time in there alone, polishing the green, unexploded World War Two hand grenade he was so fond of.

'Don't worry,' Jackson would say, 'it won't explode. Here, would you like to hold it?' He'd ask, whilst caressing the palm-sized device as though it were a fluffy, little kitten. I'd nervously decline his offer of *holding it,* just in case he was lying and decided to pull the pin.

Jackson's entire wardrobe consisted of German military gear and other wearable Nazi paraphernalia. He said he was happy to sell me his silver catapult at a knock-down price, as it was *too* modern, and didn't match the style of his other military hardware.

*This* particular deal set me back £1.50, and the *Emerson Lake and Palmer* album I'd tried so hard to like, but couldn't. We shook hands, and the catapult was mine.

According to Jackson, 'when that thing was loaded with a nicely sized rock, it was capable of knocking the wings off a low-flying buzzard at a thousand yards.' Fortunately, for the local wildlife, I never got to try it out. Within days, the eagle-eyed *Glynis* had struck again. My catapult, *and* the bottle of Guinness I'd been saving for a rainy day was gone —securely locked away with my air rifle in the main office. That evening the heavens opened, and all I could do was console myself with some warm cocoa and an early night...

I do not, however, want to give the impression

that life at Monkton was all about weaponry, alcohol and sex. In fact, we were generally quite a well behaved bunch that took pride in our temporary home. A good example of this were the compulsory school meetings.

On Mondays, Tuesdays, and Thursdays, all fifty-eight pupils, and seven staff members would squeeze into the Old Library to discuss, and then vote on whichever topic of concern had been added to the day's agenda. Issues up for discussion would range from the serious to the downright stupid.

Once someone proposed banning the uneatable *pink stuff* regularly served up at lunchtimes for dessert. No one seemed to know what it was, it was just, *the pink stuff.* This was an easy win for the proposer, and resulted in an overwhelming—*yes,* let's ban it. Even the staff agreed that it was probably against our human rights to be served food that glowed like the aftermath of a nuclear explosion in a lobster farm.

We'd also, for example, discuss fining pupils who found it necessary to burn holes in the wooden furniture, with iron pokers made red-hot in the Old Library's coal fire.

And once, following a spate of painful, two-wheeled collisions, we debated whether bicycles should be ridden clockwise, or anti-clockwise around the main building. Unfortunately, clockwise and anti-clockwise were not words I could visualise, so on this, and many other topics, I thought it best to vote for *both* sides of the argument—just in case.

The *bigger* idea behind these meetings, however, was to encourage young people to speak up for themselves. But although I quite enjoyed the weekly cut and thrust of impassioned debate, I'd often struggle to follow the arguments.

Still, I did my best to contribute a few words here and there. And to my surprise, people actually listened. Sometimes, I'd even spot the odd head nodding in agreement with my point of view.

My pre-meeting strategy was simple, practice a few short sentences that would probably fit somewhere in the debate, and deliver them as soon as it was my turn to speak. This seemed to work pretty well, although people were always telling me to, 'speak up, we can't hear you.'

Actually, people were still saying this to me well into my twenties. Getting my words *out* was one thing, but delivering them at a level any higher than a whisper was another.

These days, I appear to have gone too far the other way. And *Bonnie*—my long suffering wife—often asks why I'm speaking so loudly.

It seems that I continue to misjudge the volume of my speech. Perhaps, one day I'll overcome this problem. Till then I shall rely on the feedback of others to inform me of both the quality of my conversation, and the number of decibels projected.

## 15

## THE IMPORTANCE OF MUSIC

*For as long as I can remember, music has been both the conduit through which my emotions have travelled and the destination in which they rest.*

In 1968, my grandmother bought me a portable record player. It was the type popular at the time—housed in something that resembled a small, blue leatherette suitcase. It had a lid I kept closed when not in use, to stop dust collecting on the needle.

The record player arrived with a box full of records from an uncle who no longer wanted them. There were dozens of singles and long-players from the late 1950s and early 60s. And amongst the gems were original recordings by Elvis Presley, Buddy Holly, Frank Sinatra, Nat King Cole, Perry Como and Lonnie Donegan. A collection of classic pop from an era that has inspired musicians ever since.

Soon my musical knowledge expanded to include the songs I heard on dad's little transistor radio. The reception was not always good, but when atmospherics allowed, the background static would subside just long enough to make out the crackly sound of a new *Beatles* record, or the latest offering from those edgy young things—*The Rolling Stones.*

I'd play those records over and over again—singing along whilst bouncing up and down on my bed as though it were a sort of trampoline-stage.

Sometimes mum would shout angrily up the stairs from the kitchen:

*'STEVEN*, CAN YOU STOP JUMPING, YOU'LL COME THROUGH THE FLOOR!'

Hating conflict, I'd immediately stop bouncing, and divert my attention to the tiny text printed on the various record sleeves. I could happily spend an afternoon studying the names of who wrote the songs, who produced the records, and who played the instruments.

The sound of those melodies were mesmerising, and required nothing of me, other than to fall into their harmonious and comforting flow. I would emerge from their influence—changed, calmed, and lifted.

When Paul McCartney sang, *'fool on the hill,'* I had the distinct feeling he was talking to me. And when The Beach Boys sang, *'god only knows,'* I could feel Carl Wilson's reassuring voice reach deep into my soul to let me know everything was going to be okay.

Yet, whilst being an intimate observer of other people's music was both vital and fulfilling, nothing could connect me to my emotions like writing and playing my *own* songs on the guitar. But this would not happen until I turned twelve, and in my second year at Monkton Wyld.

## 16

## LEARNING THE PIANO: 1971

*Learning to read music is not dissimilar to learning mathematics—another skill in which I cannot progress beyond the basics.*

At the start of my third term at Monkton Wyld, I signed up for classical piano lessons with *Leslie*.

Fair-haired and petite, Leslie possessed the patience of ten saints—every ounce of which would be drained by my weekly, thirty-minute lessons…

'*Steven*, we've been practising this simple piece for weeks, and you *still* can't get past the first few bars without forgetting where you are.'

Of this stark fact I was acutely aware. But not only was I unable to remember *anything* from the previous week, I was also losing the battle to coordinate two hands and ten-fingers, whilst scanning a page of black dots and symbols that looked like small, spiky tadpoles.

'The thumb on your left hand should be playing *G* on that part, and your right index finger should be hovering over middle *C*, ready to play the melody on the next section.'

Again, Leslie would repeat her seemingly simple instructions. But she may as well have told me a thousand times in Swahili. I was just not capable of understanding her. And another frustrating lesson would end with the fruitless reminder of, 'don't forget to practise *Steven*, I hope to see some improvement by next week.'

My resistance to the idea of practising, however, was not determined only by the impossible task of synchronising brain, hand and eye. There was another significant factor stifling my progress—*the supernatural.*

I shall explain…

From the piano stool behind the school's magnificent mahogany *Bechstein*, one could see out through the Gothic-styled windows and across to the green upslope on the other side of the valley. This is a patchwork masterpiece of small fields dotted with grazing cattle, and separated into rough squares by dark hedgerows and forestry.

Whilst this view was—and still is—never short of spectacular, I could not pretend to feel comfortable in that room. I would certainly *never* enter alone. Especially after dark when the view disappeared into opaque, reflective blackness.

The Old History Room had, for some reason, become the *go-to* destination for late-night seances. These were held by a handful of foolhardy pupils for whom speaking with the dead by way of a home-made ouija board made for a *fun* extracurricular activity.

And although I did not personally witness any of this alleged occultism—others had.

In fact, it was *Spitbag* (after he'd recovered from his White Supremacist phase, and we'd become friends) who'd told me about the disembodied spirits that apparently swirled around the light bulb above the piano. He also told me about the floating-ghost-babies, and the faces of dead ex-pupils peering in through the Old History Room window.

To his credit, *Spitbag* admitted that he couldn't, with all certainty, validate these rumours, but was generally of the opinion there could be no smoke without fire.

Yet *Spitbag* was not devoid of *all* occult experience. He once told me that after downing a gallon and a half of local cider, he actually took part in one of these late-night seances in The Old History Room...

'So, *Spitbag,*' I enquired some time later, 'were you scared? Did you see anything? Did anything happen?'

'Well, after all of that cider, things were a bit

hazy,' he recalled with a vague, far away expression on his face.

'But… I do remember the table lifting into the air, and the ouija board suddenly flying across the room and crashing into the piano. Other than that… it was a bit boring really…'

But it wasn't only *Spitbag the understater* who'd witnessed unexplainable events in the Old History Room. Others had told me they'd heard paranormal excerpts of Beethoven's *Moonlight Sonata* emanating from that haunted space in the wee small hours before dawn.

False rumours they may, or may not have been, but nonetheless, sufficiently influential to dissuade me from solitary piano practice after dark.

Better to suffer the wrath of an angry *Leslie* for not perfecting that tricky piece of *Bach,* than to risk a terrifying encounter with a haunted piano.

In any case, my days as a pianist were numbered, and for entirely practical reasons.

Leslie always insisted I keep my fingernails short on both hands.

'We don't want to sound as though our fingers are tap dancing on the ivories *Steven*—do we now?' She'd say.

Conversely: *Brian*—tutor of the next instrument I would learn—insisted I keep my *left* hand nails *short*, but that my *right* hand fingernails should be:

'Long enough to shovel shit from the cowshed.' Thus, enabling efficient string-plucking.

The choice was simple. Short nails and *Leslie,* versus long nails and *Brian.*

And whilst the mental image of fingers tap dancing on the ivories was far more enticing than the one where I'm scooping up hot, brown, cow excrement with my bare hands, it was clear that in the battle of the fingernails there could only be one winner.

And unfortunately for Leslie, it would *not* be her.

## 17

# HOW I BECAME GEORGE: 1972

*There are quite possibly more people alive in this world that refer to me by my Monkton Wyld nickname George, than know me as Steve or Steven.*

I'm not sure whether it's compulsory for boarding school pupils to have their birth names morphed into humorous or—more often than not—insulting variations of those given by their parents. But the one thing I *do* know, is once a nickname reaches a critical mass of users, it's likely to stick for a *very* long time.

Fifty years on, and ageing school reunion participants continue to relive that hilarious day in 1962 when Ian *Winky* Smith was caught shagging Alice *Plonky* Rogers in the woods by History teacher, *Merv the Perv*.

'There's no smoke without Fire,' we'd remark

about *Merv's* suspiciously short-lived employment at the school.

'Perhaps I'm getting old,' says a confused *Beaky* Hawkshore, 'but I could have sworn it was *Daffers* and not *Plonky* in those bushes? Still, at our age, it's surprising we can remember *anything!'*

Everyone laughs, and the stories continue…

'And what about the time Simon *Sweaty Palms* Palmer became thirsty during the night and sneaked, naked, into the cowsheds with his torch? Then (so the story goes) he lay flat on his back under a heavily laden Friesian and squirted warm, full-fat milk into that great big gob of his.'

'Still sounds like bit of an old wives tale,' says *Stinker* cynically. '*Sweaty* always *was* a bit of a fibber if you ask me.'

Heads nod in fond agreement at shared memories now half-a-century old, and another cup of tea is taken all round.

Nicknames are, it seems, a bit like Japanese Knotweed—pervasive, and often unwanted. They creep up on you when you're not looking, and before you know it, *everyone*—even the staff—is referring to you as *George Best,* because you've got long dark hair and you're *so* good at football. Soon any trace you were ever a *Steven* has disappeared.

Even my end-of-term school reports would state:

*George has made good progress this term.*

*Oversensitive at times but generally stable. Promising guitarist. Lacks focus in class.*

I have, since, become a very proud *George*. And to ex-Monkton Wylders will remain a *George* until the day it appears in brackets under a carved *Star of David* on a gravestone somewhere in Jewish North-West London.

Life as a *George,* however, has not always been easy.

For a term or two, I suffered the indignities of being a *Georgina,* then an *Ina,* and then an *Ina Sharples,* before coming to an uneasy nickname rest as a *Hairnet*—an unfortunate iteration referring to *Ina Sharples*—the drab, hairnet wearing Northern lass of TV's longest running soap *Coronation Street.*

Once, I was a proud little *George Best,* and then, quite suddenly, and by popular consensus, I had morphed into a grubby Mancunian hair restrainer.

'Hey, *Hairnet*... wanna play football?' They'd shout at me from the far side of the public playing fields in Charmouth. Strangers would turn their heads in my direction to hear me reply, 'yeah, sure, I'll be over in a minute.' Affirming my acceptance of unfortunate nickname-creep.

Generally, my nicknames were delivered with affection and not designed to cause offence.

The exception to this, however, were a few

unpleasant weeks in 1973, when my *big fat Jewish secret* became *big fat common knowledge...*

From the day I arrived at Monkton, I'd worried about being the only Jew in an overwhelmingly white, Christian, Anglo-Saxon boarding school. And in addition, a good two hundred miles from anyone else who shared a lineage back to *Moses.* I guarded my Jewishness as though I were hiding a secret serial killer past. But then, one day, and for no apparent reason, the unlikely pairing of *Spitbag* and *Brownfinger* decided to experiment with some low-level anti-Semitism.

'*Big nosed Jew* and *stingy yid,*' they'd shout at me from a safe distance—giggling moronically like early incarnations of *Beavis and Butthead.*

At first, I wasn't too bothered by all of this. After all, I couldn't argue with the accuracy of their words. I *was* a Jew, and I *did* have a prominent—some say attractive—Jewish nose. But, for the record, I absolutely refute the allegations of being *stingy.* Careful, perhaps, but definitely not stingy.

But then, events took on an altogether more sinister tone.

One afternoon, I returned to my room on the top floor of the old house to find the wall behind my bed had been graffitied with thick black swastikas.

Or at least that's what they were *meant* to be. The shapes were all wrong. Sort of backwards and inside out. As if drawn with the aid of a mirror by a drunken, one-eyed chimp. And below the misshapen swastikas were a laughable selection of misspelt insults. Something like: *GO HOWM JUW!* And *DANJER! JUWS LIV HEAR!*

Fortunately, the unsavoury episode concluded shortly afterwards when the two literary-challenged culprits chased me along the lane and into a field, hurling insult after insult.

But then, suddenly emboldened by the courage of the ancient Israelites, I felt the fear drain from my body. I stopped in my tracks and turned to face my cowardly assailants. And then, with the look of a man intent on reaping a deadly vengeance, I sprinted back towards *Spitbag* and *Brownfinger* like a heroic knight in a mediaeval joust. '*GO AWAY,*' I screamed at them. The somewhat less than feeble *Spitbag* fell backwards onto a grassy bank to avoid my charge, and *Brown-finger* disappeared as fast as he could into the distance.

My enemies had scattered like pathetic leaves in the wind, and would not bother me again.

## 18

# LEARNING THE GUITAR: 1972

From the moment I lifted Simon's shiny new acoustic guitar from its case and plucked tentatively on those taught nylon strings, I simply knew I had to have one of my own.

By the age of thirteen, Simon had already mastered an entire classical piece by the wonderful Brazilian composer *Villa-Lobos*. Carefully, I handed the delicate instrument back to my blond Germanic roommate, and looked on in awe as he launched confidently, into the *one* tune he could play all the way through. His hands seemed to dance effortlessly across the fretboard—barely touching the strings—yet the sound that emanated was rich, melodic and deeply soothing. I was transfixed and needed more of that warm, harmonic rush.

Back home in London for the end-of-term spring break, I asked dad if he would buy me a guitar. And without a moment's hesitation, he suggested we pay a visit to Kilburn High Road's very own temple of sound: *Blanks Musical Instruments.*

The following Saturday, dad and I were browsing the rows of beautifully ornate guitars—most of which came at a price sure to cause mild palpitations in the chest of the average working class man.

Feeling a little downhearted, the assistant pointed dad and I in the direction of the *affordable* section, and at once a happy number of possibilities sprung forth.

We finally settled on a reasonably priced classical guitar with a decent sound. The assistant wrapped the instrument in clear polythene, and dad handed over the nine pounds of hard earned cash he'd expertly negotiated down from ten. I then raced home as fast as I could to try it out.

'Look, mum, look what I've got,' I called out— ripping open the plastic wrapping to reveal the most beautiful thing I'd ever seen.

'That's nice dear, careful you don't break it!' She replied with her usual exaggerated sense that if something *could* go wrong, it probably would. But I was *way* too excited to indulge in any such negativity, and in extra quick time, my new guitar was released from its protective shell—ready to be strummed and admired.

I doubt whether that curvaceous piece of carved and laminated wood was out of my hands for more than a few waking hours during those first few months. If I wasn't playing my new best *friend*, I was gently massaging furniture polish into its exquisite form, or tweaking its silver-plated tuning pegs at the slightest hint of an out of tune string.

In fact, so besotted was I with my new guitar, that within days I could play a few simple melodies, and within weeks I'd learnt enough chords to write my first song—a quaint little ditty in the style of Buddy Holly entitled: *Will You Always Be True*. I'd play it to mum and my ten-year-old sister in the kitchen whilst the chicken soup was boiling away on the stove.

*'If I was to say to you, will you always be true…'* I'd sing in my high, unbroken voice—pretending I was The Beatles at Madison Square Garden.

'Hmm… that's a nice song dear,' mum would say —attempting to hide her embarrassment by clearing her throat several times before daring to enquire any further.

'Is it… err… is it about someone you know at… err… Monkton Wyld *Steven*?' She'd *just* about ask. No doubt hoping I wouldn't explain in *too* much detail, what had inspired such surprisingly adult-themed lyrics.

She needn't have worried, I was too young to understand what I'd written about. Although I must admit, the verse about the girl with the long blond hair at the previous year's Christmas party was pretty close to the truth. But then, I was a Monkton Wylder.

And things happen at boarding school that never *could* in a month of local, state-comprehensive-Sundays.

Finally, the holidays came to an end, and I returned to school, eager to sign up for lessons with *Brian*—the school's bearded, antipodean guitar teacher.

Brian approached life with the easygoing style of an optimistic surfer dude. Qualities, no doubt, honed on a succession of sunny southern hemisphere beaches as a teenager.

'Come on *George*… you can do it,' he'd say encouragingly whenever I was stuck on a particularly difficult section of *Bach, or Tarrega*, or my other favourite composer—some guy by the name of *TRAD*.

*TRAD* was so famous, that like *Castro, Churchill* and *Gandhi,* first names were deemed superfluous. It was not until the following year that Brian—in his humorous Australian twang—finally informed me that the remarkably gifted and prolific *TRAD* was not actually a person. And that, any piece of music attributed to *TRAD,* simply referred to a song that had been passed down through the generations *uncredited*. The way folk music often is.

So, what about my other favourite *one-name* composer: *ANON?* I enquired sheepishly.

'No mate… *not* a person either, it just means that no one knows who the f***ing composer was…

surely *everyone* knows that, *mate?!*' Obvious really, when you think about it. But then, I'm autistic and *nothing* has ever been particularly obvious to me.

With these, and a few other blindingly obvious misconceptions cleared up by the all-knowing Brian, guitar lessons continued to good effect. And driven by the impassioned single-mindedness with which I pursue *every* obsessive interest, my string plucking progress leapt exponentially forward at a pace that surprised even Brian.

## My First Gig

The first time I played to an audience other than mum and my sister in the kitchen, was at the Monkton Wyld end-of-term concert.

I was thirteen, and so overcome with fear that I turned my chair to face the back of the stage—thus avoiding the gaze of a hundred sets of expectant young eyes.

With my guitar clamped firmly by trembling hands, I counted myself into the song Brian had been teaching me for weeks: *Oh Suzanna...*

'*Oh Suzanna, won't you marry me? Coz I come from Alabama with a banjo on my knee...*'

But having successfully negotiated the first verse and chorus, things started to go *wrong—badly* wrong.

The sickening familiarity of mental disconnect began to wash over me in wave after disabling wave.

Suddenly, I could not remember a single thing about the song. In fact, I couldn't even remember which song I was playing!

Unable to find my way back to the correct chord sequence, I somehow managed to improvise a ramshackle collection of *wrong* notes that—for the first time in its history—propelled *Oh Suzanna* into the unpleasant atonal realms of spontaneous avant-garde Jazz. My somewhat unusual version of *Oh Suzanna* finished on a strangely unresolved chord that left everyone—including me—unsure as to whether the the song had actually ended.

I remained in my seat facing the back wall of the stage wondering what, if anything, I should do next. Until, thankfully, the uncomfortable silence was finally broken by a loud antipodean *whoop* from Brian. 'Bravo *mate… Bravo…'* He shouted from the wings. A short round of applause from the generally confused audience lasted just long enough to accompany my exit from the stage.

'Don't worry mate, we all forget the words some-times,' said Brian sympathetically.

But inside I knew that *forgetting* things, was just one part of my problem. Remembering things in the *first* place would provide an even greater barrier to my future success.

I cannot fully describe how memory loss has blighted every aspect of my life. Songs do not get any simpler than the three-chord *Oh Suzanna*. Yet even this had slipped through the fingers of my cognitive grasp like water through a sieve.

My initialisation into the world of live performance that night was merely the shape of things to come. A career in music defined by burning ambition and the cruel disconnect of mental dysfunction.

A battle I could not ultimately win.

## 19

# GOLF: MY OCD HELL

*There's something deeply satisfying about launching that tiny white ball high into a clear blue sky. To watch it fly, and land on a perfect patch of lush grass somewhere in the distance.*

Why, from the age of seven I became so obsessed with the game of golf is a mystery. The bookshelves above my bed positively groaned under the weight of golfing self-tuition manuals offering tips like: *How to Swing like Arnold Palmer*, and *How to Hit the Perfect Shot Every Time.*

But, I never did learn how to translate this invaluable literary advice into real-world improvements. In fact, it turns out the books had lied. It's just not possible to hit the *perfect* shot every time. Perhaps a book entitled: *How to Avoid Snakes Whilst Searching for Your Golf Ball in The Long Grass,* would have been a more useful addition to my overflowing library of sport. But more on snakes later.

Until I'd become a pupil at Monkton Wyld, my golfing passions were indulged at Horsingdon Hill—a small public course not far from home.

On Sundays, when work and money allowed, dad would take me there for a round of golf. Or more accurately, an afternoon spent hunting for one of his miss-hit golf balls buried somewhere deep in the long grass.

A round of golf with dad was not unlike an off-route nature ramble through the Amazon rainforest. A hopeless scramble through dense undergrowth from which we would invariably emerge fifteen-minutes later with *someone else's* lost ball.

Often, dad's shots were so wayward, it was not immediately obvious which hole he was actually playing.

Was he searching through those knee-high brambles because he'd strayed from the short-fourth between the tall pine trees and the out-of-bounds on the left? Or, because he'd attempted an ambitious three-iron on the long *seventh*—a feat normally undertaken only by the really *good* players or the foolhardy, not so good ones.

I once saw dad take a mighty swing off the first

tee. I watched his ball slice diagonally across the fairway, hit a nearby boundary fence post with a loud metallic *clunk*, and rebound with force, directly back to where he was standing. Instinctively, he ducked, and the ball continued on its bizarre trajectory behind him.

The ball was finally brought to a safe, but shattering halt against the expansive glass frontage of the newly renovated clubhouse.

This was the most remarkably freakish shot ever to have been played off the first-tee at Horsingdon Hill. And quite possibly *ever, anywhere,* in the long and illustrious history of the game. The balding clubhouse manager, however, had not appreciated dad's accidental genius, and ran out to inspect the damage to his window. Dad shrugged his shoulders as if to say, *did that really just happen?*

Fortunately, the crack was no more than a couple of feet in diameter. And after the angry manager had suggested that, 'a couple of lessons may a good idea,' dad and I headed off up the fairway towards my perfectly hit ball resting proudly, a few feet from the flag.

Dad would say:

'It's not about hitting perfect shots *Steven*. It's about the two of us being out here on the course having fun, and enjoying each other's company.'

But I wasn't impressed by his *laissez-faire* approach to golf.

As with *everything* I do, I have an unhealthy need to be brilliant. To be *better* than everyone else.

Forget all that *smell the roses along the way* stuff. On the golf course I want to be Tiger Woods, and on the guitar I want to be Eric Clapton. Anything less means I'm a complete failure—there *is* no in-between.

* * *

I take a moment to consider the possibility that this unforgiving state of mind is, in fact, the symptom of a self-destructive circular process.

A lack of self-esteem drives the need for perfection. And when this perfection is not met, a further tainting of self image generates an even greater need to impress. And so the negative spiral continues…

## Golf and OCD: Age Thirteen

The exhausting compulsions that first entered my psyche on the football field a few years earlier, had now followed me onto the golf course.

To his credit, dad would stand patiently by—without comment or criticism—waiting for my extensive pre-shot routine to end.

Depending on my anxiety levels that day, I could easily spend five-minutes readying myself before taking a shot. Everything in my body had to *feel* perfect before I could lift the golf club to begin the backswing.

I'd need to *swallow* either twice, four times, or eight times whilst holding on to a certain mental image. This would always be in combination with a specific piece of music.

If, during my practice swing, I accidentally brushed the right side of my face with my shoulder, I would need to brush it again to make it an *even* number, and then balance this by brushing the *other* side of my face an equal number of times.

Sometimes I'd become so trapped inside the paralysing grip of nervous tics, counting rituals and mental contamination, that I would have to walk away and start again.

Backtracking for a moment, I should add that *mental contamination* is a type of OCD. It means that I find it extremely distressing to perform an action if I have an unpleasant mental image in my mind. If I cannot clear this *infecting* image before I begin a task, something terrible will happen.

Of course, it won't really. It's just my disabling blend of OCD, autism and anxiety that creates such catastrophic thinking.

Fifty years on, and still the destructive curse of Obsessive Compulsive Disorder continues to add infinite layers of complexity to the simplest of daily tasks. Yet, the treatment for the condition does not appear to have changed greatly over the years.

Doctors claim to have had good outcomes from the combination of antidepressants and Cognitive Behavioural Therapy. But CBT is unlikely to work for those of us with communication, and language processing disorders.

Cognitive Behavioural Therapy relies on the ability of the patient to change their thinking. To create new mental pictures. And to realise a situation could have a different outcome from the distressing one they've grown accustomed to.

Unfortunately, the communication and social imagination skills necessary for CBT to be effective, are weak in people with autism. And in addition, many of us are also hindered by inflexible thinking. This factor alone renders traditionally delivered CBT unhelpful to people on the spectrum.

Clearly, a different approach is needed. Mental health services need to develop the flexibility and expertise to adjust for people with autism, and other developmental disorders. It's simply not good enough to ignore the emotional wellbeing of an entire section of society.

My rant concludes—for now.

Lets get back to the reason I'm so obsessed by the game of golf...

## 20

## GOLF: THE PATH TO
## ENLIGHTENMENT

During my second year as a Monkton Wylder, I accepted the exciting opportunity to become immersed in the noble art of golf on a much grander scale.

In the spring of 1972, at the age of thirteen, I officially became the second youngest member of *Lyme Regis Golf Club*. The youngest being my Monkton Wyld roommate *Bruce.*

Each week, I'd walk the three-miles from Monkton to the course at Lyme. This was a tiring journey along steep country lanes—made even more exhausting by the weighty bag of golf clubs I'd carry over my shoulder.

On arrival, I'd see, over to my right, a handful of posh cars belonging to the club's senior members. They were parked in the spaces reserved for well-heeled local defenders of the realm, and had names like:

- *(Club Treasurer) Sir William Winthrop-Thorpe.*
- *(Committee Chairman) Major Philip Harrison-Brown OBE.*
- *(Men's Team Captain) The RT Hon. James Wentworth-Stuffington-Smythe.*

That gorgeous green outpost of little England was my holy land. A perfect eighteen-hole course perched high and precariously on the crumbling cliffs above Lyme Bay. And after my weekly, hour's tuition with *Jack Hoare*—the club's legendary golf professional—I'd venture out alone across the vast windswept course for another five-hours of supreme golfing adventure.

The highlight of each round at Lyme was always the fifteenth-fairway that ran along the high, sandstone cliff edge. A few too many steps to the left whilst playing from the long grass, and one could easily fall to a certain death in the crashing waves hundreds of feet below. Sometimes, I'd become so overwhelmed and light-headed by the enormity of it all, that I'd have to step away in case I was tempted to hurl myself over the edge, in self-sacrifice to one of God's mightiest creations.

From here, one is also captivated by the awe-inspiring view of *Golden Cap* rising up from the beach to become the highest sea cliff on Britain's Jurassic south coast—a bright, natural beacon for ships traversing the choppy waters of Lyme bay.

Whether spring, summer, autumn or winter, the view out over the sea was immense and spectacular. A constantly changing work of art—untamed and perfect. The fickle ecosystem that seemed to apply only to the fifteenth-fairway, could, within a matter of minutes, allow a thick sea mist to descend and restrict visibility to just a few yards. Alternatively, the turbulent coastal breeze may decide to whip itself into an invisible barrier to any ball hit high into the air—changing its direction and stalling its progress.

By way of contrast, and far from the sound of crashing waves, other parts of the course weaved their way elegantly between the Oak and Birch of fine English woodland. Here, all that could be heard were the sounds of insects, and the occasional disembodied voice of an unseen golfer screaming apologetically: *'FORRR... ON THE LEFT.'* A woody-crack of ball against breaking-branch would echo briefly through the trees, followed by a loud, *'SORRY,'* to the players up ahead who'd narrowly escaped a ball to the head.

Playing golf at Lyme Regis, however, was not without an altogether darker side—as club professional *Jack Hoare* frequently reminded me in his strong West Country accent:

'Mind you don't go too near the cliff edge on the fifteenth-fairway—Lord knows how many members we've lost over there this past year!'

And during the warm weather months, *Jack* would say:

'Never put your hand in the brambles to retrieve your ball.'

Because…

'You'll find all manner of snakes in those bushes, and Lord knows how many members we've lost to snake bites this season!'

There seemed to be lots of things *The Lord* knew that Jack didn't. Perhaps, putting the fear of God into me before I set out on a round of golf was Jack's way of showing he cared. After all, I was only thirteen, and if I *did* happen to fall over the dangerous unfenced cliffs on the fifteenth-fairway, I would have almost certainly met my death on the rocky shoreline below.

And as for Jack's dire warning about Britain's only deadly snake—the mildly poisonous *Adder* —well, I can only recall *one* unfortunate member falling victim to its venom. This was a retired local businessman who was nipped in the brambles on the short-eleventh whilst retrieving his ball with an ungloved hand. He consequently died from a heart attack.

According to Bruce, 'the *old duffer* was probably on his way out anyway.'

So—we concluded—no harm done really.

## The Autistic Golfer

Why do I consider golf to be such an autism-friendly sport? Well just think about it for a moment...

What could be more enjoyable for a sensitive autistic soul like me, than to spend the day alone, and away from all the noise and hassle of a complex, neurotypical world?

Surely, there is *no* other sport that ticks my autistic boxes the way golf can. Although, I suppose it could be argued that *fishing* shares the potential for a peaceful afternoon of sport in the countryside.

But, I am not a fan of fishing. Just imagine you're strolling along the local high street one day when suddenly, an enticing McDonald's quarter pounder falls from the sky.

As you sink your teeth into the juicy burger, you feel the sharp pain of a large metal hook attaching itself to your left ear. Suddenly, you feel a violent *tug* hoisting you skywards above everything you've ever known—never to be seen again...

I do not consider the killing of fish to be an activity free from anxiety. Even if it *does* usually take place in an idyllic location.

But again, I digress. This is *not* a book about fishing, I just get a little sidetracked sometimes…

Getting back to the subject of *golf*. I would like to end this chapter by saying that I've always found the *playing* of it to be a curious combination of pleasure, *and* frustration. But then this can be said about life in general. Sometimes, the harder you try, the worse things get. But you keep on trying anyway in the hope you may achieve something great one day.

Playing golf at Lyme Regis was not just about hitting a little white ball towards a distant flag. The beauty of that sporting paradise held me in the arms of something much *bigger*—mystical, and quite different to anything I'd experienced before.

Out on that wild and windy course, I was at one with nature, the seasons, and the great expanse of open sky that joined land and sea. For the first time in my life I felt powerful, free and connected. I could finally claim my place in the *cosmic* grand scheme of things.

At Lyme Regis Golf Club, I was at home, and I was at peace.

## 21

## IN HOSPITAL AGAIN: 1972

*Only those who have faced the indescribable mental pain of clinical depression can know of its paralysing, and unrelenting despair.*

The spring end-of-term break drew to a close, and the day had arrived to leave, once again, the safe comfort of home, for the cold, chiselled sandstone of Monkton Wyld.

*'TIME TO GET UP NOW!'* I heard mum call from the bottom of the stairs. 'It's 9 am. Don't forget you're going back to school today.'

I peeked out from under the covers to see my old brown suitcase standing upright and packed—ready for the train journey back to school that afternoon.

Mum was now standing by my bed, urging me to get up… 'Come on now *Steven*, get yourself washed and dressed—we'll have to leave for the station soon.'

How was I ever going to convince her that I was too unwell to even *think* about making the trip back to school that day?

But I was not unwell because I had the flu or a heavy cough, or an easily provable dose of Chicken Pox. In fact, I didn't exactly know *why* I felt so ill. I simply assumed that anything other than a toothache had something to do with not being a *normal* child.

I closed my eyes and tunnelled deeper under the covers—praying for the sleep from which I would not wake.

From beneath my sheets I could just hear mum on the kitchen phone:

*'He simply won't get out of bed doctor—I honestly don't know what to do with him anymore.'*

Mum was using her special telephone voice. It was that same reverential, yet exasperated tone she'd *always* use when speaking about *me* to someone important. Like a doctor or a social worker:

*'Okay then, I'll try one more time.'* I heard her say.

Moments later, mum was back, standing by my bedroom door…

'They said you've got to get up *now* Steven. If you hurry you'll just catch the later train to Monkton Wyld. Otherwise you'll get in trouble and end up in hospital again!'

But I was falling deeper and deeper into the unreachable mental space that engulfs me like calm quicksand whenever I'm severely distressed.

Soon the train on which I *should* have been travelling would have left London with its noisy cargo of boisterous, boarding school teenagers. *My* destination however, would be much closer to home.

The following morning, a black London taxi pulled up outside our house. Above the distinctive mechanical rattle of its chugging diesel engine, the cheerful cockney driver asks mum:

'Where to *love*?'

'Great Ormond Street Hospital, please cabbie.'

* * *

This particular spell in hospital was my longest ever —somewhere around three months. It was also my first time in the new child psychiatry annexe—built especially for children like me. Whatever *that* meant.

I was not, however, expecting this change of hospital venue, and my stomach began to churn with worry at the thought of something new and unexpected happening. In fact, I hated *any* kind of change. And in order to seek reassurance, I would fire a thousand-and-one questions at the nearest responsible adult: 'How long will it take to get there…? Do they know about my problems? Will mum know where I am…?' I asked the nurse who showed me around the new ward.

According to dad, I was one of the first children to be admitted into the new child psychiatric wing—a sort of one-stop-fixing-shop for the *educationally subnormal*, the *emotionally disturbed*, and any other generally *abnormal* child whose unusual behaviour was deemed beyond classification.

My new temporary home was a vision of sparse 1970s functionality. Unfussy, clean, and modern. Instead of the old style multi-bed wards, I shared a good-sized double bedroom with another *abnormal* boy called Timothy.

The new unit was also a day centre, where less *disturbed* children attended as outpatients. Together we were tutored by specialist staff in fresh white rooms overlooking Russell Square's towering trees. Here I would draw pictures and write stories about my feelings. Dr Howarth—the psychiatrist who'd sent me to Monkton Wyld—would ask, during my weekly visits to his office:

'Those pictures you drew this morning *Steven*, why do you suppose they were so full of dark clouds?'

And:

'Is there any particular reason you're not able to look at me, *Steven?* What is it over *there* you find so fascinating…?'

Having neither the language skills to explain how

I felt, or the self-awareness to understand my motivations, I'd shrug my shoulders and ask the only question that mattered: *'When can I go home…?'*

## Timothy

Even by *my* standards, Timothy seemed *odd*. Firstly, he did not speak a single word the whole six weeks we were roommates. And most of the time he appeared utterly lost to the world—unreachable and self-absorbed. He'd just sit in the chair next to his bed until a nurse came along and told him to do something. Like:

'Go to the toilet *Timothy*.'

Or…

'Go and get your lunch *Timothy*.'

The other unusual thing about Timothy was that he found it impossible to enter the room without flicking the light switch on and off, and on and off again, at least a dozen times. The sound of that constantly clicking light switch was enough to make me explode with rage. I'd put my hands over my ears and scream, *'STOP DOING THAT!'* Yet, however loud I shouted, he just carried on flicking the switch as if I were invisible to him.

Depending on the time of day, a nurse would come along to dispense either my Lithium or my Valium. I didn't know what it was at the time, or why I was taking it, but I knew those pills were not making me feel any *better*—just really, really tired. And as though I were becoming increasingly detached from my surroundings. I remember once at visiting time, mum was busy chatting away to one of the other mothers when something made me lurch violently across the table. I sunk my fingers into the side of a boy's face and squeezed until his face was bright red and bleeding. He cried out in pain until hospital staff were finally able to wrench my hand from his cheek.

Unsurprisingly, my random attack on the unfortunate boy did not go unnoticed by the doctors, and shortly after the incident I overheard mum say to a nurse:

'They just don't know what to do with him anymore. The doctor said he's considering something called *ECT* (Electro-Convulsive Therapy) but isn't that dangerous...?'

Thankfully, Dr Howarth decided against attempting to spark some *normality* into my thirteen-year-old-brain by plugging me into the National Power Grid. He must have known that within a week or so, the Lithium would've flattened me out and turned me off *anyway!*

\* \* \*

Timothy left the hospital after a number of annoying light-switch-flicking-weeks. This left me as sole occupier of the double room. Dad brought my guitar up to the hospital, and I busied myself learning, and then instantly forgetting, the chords to all the current hits of the day:

*Puppy Love* by Donny Osmond, *Starman* by David Bowie, and *Vincent* by Don McLean.

I left hospital some weeks later, a much improved guitarist, and ever so slightly healed from the worst of my depression.

But soon, the universe would throw me into the whirlwind of a scandal that set local tongue's wagging like never before…

## 22

## SCANDAL

'Sex Diary Found at School!'

Convalescing at home after my release from the psych ward, my attention was brought to the headline printed large in mum's copy of the Daily Mirror:

> *Dorset police say they have uncovered a revealing sex diary at a boarding school in Dorset.*
>
> *The diary was found yesterday during a high profile drugs raid at Monkton Wyld School. A number of pupils have been charged with possession of Cannabis…*

In shock, I rushed out into the garden to tell mum. She was already engaged in a heated debate over the garden fence with the usually tight-lipped (at least, with mum) Mrs White. Obviously, Mrs White had already seen the article and simply couldn't resist asking:

'Isn't that the school your *Steven* goes to *Mrs Slavin*?'

Mum probably replied:

'Yes, Mrs White, but I'm sure my Steven had nothing to do with the drugs or the sex-diary. In any case, he's been in hospital for months, how could he *possibly* be involved…?'

But mums stout defence would do little to stem the flow of rumours spreading like Chinese-whispered-wildfire from one end of Grasmere Avenue to the other. By the time the news had reached the warped ear of Mrs Brownlow at number *28,* the *Slavins* were a family of heroin-addicted, child-sacrificing Zionists—bent on corrupting the entire neighbourhood.

Whilst mum continued to deal with the aftermath of the biggest scandal ever to rock Grasmere Avenue, I returned to Monkton to find my personal items had been tampered with during the police raid. My Jethro Tull and Pink Floyd albums were strewn irreverently across my bed. And even worse, my personal stash of instant coffee granules had been tipped out and left to congeal into hundreds of sticky little brown lumps on the shelf.

Apparently, the police arrived on mass with dogs, and had left no stone unturned in their search for evidence of illegal activity. Yet, despite their best efforts, all the enthusiastic boys-in-blue found was Harriet's (probably inaccurate) sex diary—and the tiniest piece of hash belonging to one of the older boys.

Later that year, a TV film crew came to Monkton to make a documentary—obviously hoping to cash in on the wave of publicity following the drugs raid.

When the film aired nationally a few months later, it may have stoked the smouldering fires of Grasmere Avenue's hair-triggered, curtain twitchers for a day or two. But happily, the locals soon returned to their usual low-level mutterings about the unnatural shape and size of Mr Dobson's carrots…

'I can't imagine *what* he puts on those things—it's just not decent!' They'd all agree with feigned disgust.

But I was growing up, and beginning to care just a little less each day about the petty suburban chatter. My attention was now consumed by girls, and music, and pondering one's future through the distorted lens of early adolescent naivety. Teenage angst was the order of the day, and I guzzled from its tortured cup with the tenacious recklessness of a hopeless alcoholic.

## 23

# THE AUTISTIC HIPPIE

In 1975, my hair tumbled down over my shoulders like a crazy wild bush—sprouting forth in every direction.

I'd always wanted my hair to be dead straight, and very long like the *cool* guys at Monkton.

Pulling hard on the ends did nothing to change its natural waviness. It simply sprung back into the same tangled mess it had been before. Once, I even considered tying weights to the ends for a day or two—to help straighten it out. But the *cool* guys said this was a stupid idea, adding how much they'd like to swap some of my curls, for some of their boring straightness.

Still, hair length wasn't everything. My threadbare, extra wide, bell-bottomed *Levi's* with patches covering holes in other patches, more than adequately demonstrated my exemplary hippie credentials.

I was fifteen going on sixteen, and my hormones raged uncontrollably to the sound of 1970s rock, and the harmonious ramblings of thoughtful West Coast singer-songwriters. I'd spend hours alone in my bedroom writing songs on my guitar about the girls I could never *have,* and the dreams that may never be fulfilled.

I derived my inspiration from bands and artists like *Crosby Stills Nash* and *Young, Traffic, James Taylor* and *Joni Mitchell.*

These were the golden years before people started saying, '*we've heard it all before.'* Back then, there *wasn't* a before. Just Elvis and Sinatra, Johnny Cash and Duke Ellington.

And before music became portable on small, battery-powered devices, I carried my favourite songs around in my head. My well-stocked internal jukebox insured that a soaring *Carlos Santana* guitar solo, or nasal James Taylor melody was only ever a comforting thought away. When The Doobie Brothers sang *Listen to The Music*—I did. And when blues-rock singer Greg Allman cried out with impassioned southern grit: '*Sometimes I feel, like I've been tied, to the whipping-post...'* I felt as though I were standing next to *Greg* as the pain of unrequited love ripped mercilessly though our kindred spirits.

At night I'd drift towards sleep with Carole King's *you've got a friend* revolving gently on the turntable.

Carole really *did* make me feel as though she was my friend—the perfect kind of friend. The type that seeks nothing from me and slides conveniently back into a cardboard sleeve whenever I needed to be alone.

But as George Harrison once said, 'all things must pass.' And by the summer of 1976, my idealistic musical landscape had begun to change. The new members of Monkton Wyld's eccentric family were arriving from London with short, spiky hair—dyed orange, pink and blue. And their music sounded out of context, cold and disruptive. Yes, *Punk* had arrived at Monkton Wyld and was spewing its vulgar, urban cynicism all over my precious hippie dream.

I hated this new expression of youthful aggression. Where were the timeless melodies and the wailing guitar solos? Where were the long-haired gods of rock and the inspirational lyrics that spoke of, *'building myself a log cabin in the woods?'* Thank you *James Taylor.*

In my imagination, it was still 1970, and I clung ferociously to the traditional hippie values of peace, love and hallucinogenics as though they were going out of fashion—as, in fact, they were.

And in further defiance of those sadly changing times, my bell-bottomed Levi's grew wider, and my hair expanded to become an even bigger impenetrable mess. I, for one, was not about to let the ugly culture of *punk rock*, or any *other* trashy trend curdle my musical cream.

One day, I would—without even the slightest shadow of a long-haired doubt—strum my way to that great gig in a wondrous sky.

Thank you, *Pink Floyd*.

# 24

## DAVE

*There are autistics among us that may never know of their condition.*

David J was the *real deal*. Monkton Wyld's very own authentic all-American long-hair. A blonde escapee from a Led Zeppelin album cover who could say the word, '*man,*' without sounding fake.

*Dave* or *DJ,* as he quickly became known, was one of several young Americans who'd crossed the Atlantic to sample a slice of the Monkton Wyld magic.

A native of Philadelphia, Dave's father had been a leading academic, and his contribution to the world of science would later be honoured in a full page obituary in the *New York Times.*

Dave also had a famous rock star brother back in the States, and was, himself, an accomplished drummer. So when I discovered that Dave's drum kit had just been shipped over from Philadelphia, I excitedly suggested we form a band. And so, with the addition of Mick on bass guitar, the prog rock phenomenon known as *Quasimodo* was born.

I wouldn't, for a second, suggest we were anything special, but we sure made a hell of a racket in the Old History room each night until bedtime.

We were a kind of *Black Sabbath* meets *The Grateful Dead*, meets early *Genesis*, meets my angsty songs. But after a number of feedback squealing, cymbal crashing months, *Spitbag* broke the painful news that we were probably the worst band he'd ever heard, and pleaded with me to go *solo*...

'It's Mick and Dave–they're holding you back *George*!'

'But you're wrong *Spitbag,*' I'd reply defiantly, 'we're gonna be *big* one day—even *Brownfinger* said that from a distance we sounded just like early Led Zeppelin!'

I didn't mention that the smirking *Brownfinger* hadn't actually defined what he'd meant by, *'from a distance...'*

But eventually I bowed to public pressure and left *Quasimodo* to go solo—blaming the split on, 'musical differences,' just like Eric Clapton did when he left the supergroup *Cream*.

Thankfully, the demise of *Quasimodo* did not affect my friendships with Dave or Mick.

In fact, I continued to spend many an hour enjoying Dave's somewhat unusual musings on the world. Musings that were often made even more hilarious when lubricated by the odd gallon local cider.

I'd not met anyone like Dave before. He possessed an almost encyclopaedic knowledge of a great many things. Even if—should the truth be told —a great many slightly *odd* things.

Among his interests were:

*The relative merits of metal compounds used in the manufacture of competing drum cymbal brands.*

And…

The unrelated, yet strangely fascinating topic of *exotic teas of the world—and how to consume them for maximum taste.*

The latter of Dave's diverse range of special interests would inspire him to create the now legendary *Tea Appreciation Society of West Dorset.* Members of this exclusive club numbered just four. We'd sit around a small table on the top terrace at Monkton whilst Dave taught us everything there was to know about *Earl Grey, Lapsang Souchong, Ceylon and Darjeeling.*

Dave was a stickler for the rules of etiquette, and would become strangely agitated if the water being poured onto the delicate leaves was more than a degree under, or, a degree over the ideal temperature for the perfect brew.

He would initiate long, and often heated debates on whether it was good manners to *dunk* one's chocolate digestive in a cup of Orange Pekoe, and whether tea should be stirred in accordance with the earths rotation, or otherwise, and if the inventor of that little white bag on a string was, in fact, an evil genius, or simply a visionary, who'd sneaked an exclusive peek into the future of hot beverage consumption.

Of course, if Google had existed back then, these questions would have been answered the moment we'd obtained a decent *Wi-Fi* signal.

But are we really better off living in an age where so much low quality information can be gained instantly at the push of a virtual button?

I think not.

The fact that we never *did* find out who invented the tea bag, was, in the end, quite irrelevant. Of infinitely greater importance are those wonderful memories of sweet *Earl Grey,* and the Grateful Dead's *American Beauty* turning gently on the turntable until the sun went down on another perfect Monkton Wyld afternoon.

It would be easy to dismiss Dave's eccentricities as merely the consequence of taking a *trip* back in '74 and never quite coming back. And whilst I'd agree that LSD is unlikely to induce positive outcomes in the executive functioning department, I would suggest that undiagnosed autism may also be a factor in his less than typical view of the world.

My oldest friend *Dave* continues to be a well intentioned soul for whom life teeters constantly on the edge of some minor disaster. And I feel an obligation to protect him from the people that would take advantage of his vulnerabilities. But in all honesty, most of the time I'm just too busy trying to protect *myself* from the people that would take advantage of mine. Nonetheless, I will always be there for him—as I know he will be for *me*.

I'm happy to report that in 2018, Dave's knowledge of fine teas—both *bagged* and *loose*—is as impressive as it was in 1975.

It's good to know that some things will never change.

## 25

# FIRST LOVE: JANUARY 1976

*Social interaction: 'Difficulty in reading other people's intentions, their feelings and their needs.'*

Katy arrived at Monkton in the autumn of 1975.

She had olive skin, long dark hair, and a soft, Southern Californian accent that flowed like the finest honey.

Katy, along with a dozen or so other kids, arrived on mass from another boarding school that had suddenly been forced to close. This was, I found out just recently, something to do with a teacher who'd committed a string of murders in the US. The resulting scandal had sent the school tumbling into terminal financial decline, and Monkton had agreed to accept the fleeing pupils.

It's mind-blowing to think that if it hadn't been

for that crazed 1970s serial killer, I would never have met Katy, or indeed, Jasper—her beloved pet rat.

Also, if it hadn't been for that serial killer, I would never have met Katy, lost Katy, attempted suicide, become a Buddhist (for about six months) joined a Punk-Funk band, got a record deal in America, met Bonnie, conceived two daughters, produced music for a Heinz *Big Chunky Soup* advert and discovered I was autistic.

How strange and unpredictable life can be when you say *yes* to every opportunity that comes your way…

I hadn't really noticed Katy before. She was just one of the new kids—yet to make their mark. But all of that was about to change…

It was a cold winter's evening in the dining room, when synchronicity dictated our eyes should meet whilst simultaneously pulling our pieces of burnt bread from the four-slot, stainless steel toaster.

'I hear you're good on the guitar. Perhaps you could show me a few chords sometime?' She asked in provocative American tones.

'How about *now*,' I suggested.

Katy and I adjourned to my room on the top floor of the old house, where I showed her the first few chords of *South City Midnight Lady* by The Doobie

Brothers, and before I knew it, we were an inseparable, long-haired, denim-clad, item.

I loved everything about Katy. From her relaxed Californian style, to the way she rolled the *R* when she said *George*—my, by then, long-established nickname. I even pretended to love *Jasper*—Katy's large pet rat. He was white, and could often be found scuttling around on the bookshelf by her bed. In general, I'm not a big fan of rodents, they give me the creeps. But Jasper was *Katy's* rodent, so he was fine by me.

By the time spring 1976 arrived to warm the clear Dorset air, the pupils of Monkton Wyld had grown accustomed to referring to us in the plural:

'Has anyone seen *George and Katy*?'

And during those warm, lazy afternoons after lessons, we'd sit and talk for hours below the towering Monterey Pines that reached high above the main school building. She'd tell me about California, and I'd tell her about my dreams of becoming a famous rock musician one day. It was magical, scary and new. These were feelings I'd not experienced before. This does not mean that subsequent relationships have not been important—far from it. Nothing can top what I have with my wife Bonnie. But first relationships are often just so huge and powerful that there is always a little part of us that continues to wonder *what if?*

What if? I'd had the emotional intelligence to cope with all of those complicated thoughts and feelings? And, what if I hadn't so completely and catastrophically misread something she'd said, and told her to 'F*** OFF' in front of the entire school...?

* * *

It was a sunny Thursday afternoon, and The Old Library was filling with pupils and teachers for the weekly school meeting. I looked up to see Katy enter the room. She spotted me and instantly her face widened into a warm smile. But as she approached, I remembered that I was angry with her for some reason, and felt a sudden, overwhelming urge to get *even*.

Katy was now within touching distance, and as she opened her arms to embrace me, I summoned every ounce of force my social dysfunction could muster and screamed, *'F**K OFF!'*

Momentarily, the room quietened and heads turned to see the smile drop from her face faster than a relationship falling off a cliff. Without saying a word, she turned and walked away—no doubt wondering what on earth she could have done to inspire such anger in me. Of course, Katy had not done *anything* wrong. It was just *me* again overre-acting to a misinterpreted event earlier that day. And in those three, short seconds of undiagnosed autistic madness I had humiliated her, and triggered a violent, self-destructive storm that would rage in me for almost three years.

The extraordinary heat of June and July had broken all records, and it was not long before the school's already fragile water supply had dried to a few drops from a rusty Victorian tap.

The more hygienic amongst us took to bathing in the tumbling stream at the bottom of the valley. But to reach it, one first had to negotiate the steep, bumpy field in which a small herd of resting cows shared their space with a noisy gathering of highly strung chickens. The prize for completing this strenuous journey, however, was to splash around in the cool clear water as it cut a fast path over rocks and fallen trees to the Charmouth coast three miles away.

By way of contrast, the view from my top floor-bedroom window revealed acres of dying crops—stalk-like and distorted like a desert mirage rising and twisting above a hard-baked earth.

Day after smouldering day, the summer's unrelenting heat stifled every breath and evaporated my emotional resolve until it was gone. I wanted desperately to rekindle my relationship with Katy but she was beyond reach. I'd catch the odd glimpse of her around the school, but she had become little more than a beautiful stranger in blue denim—casting her thoughts on pastures new in distant Californian lands.

I would have gladly sold my soul to the devil for another chance to be with her. Unfortunately, or perhaps fortunately depending on how you see it, the devil never gave me this option. Instead, he tormented me like never before—plunging me into the depths of a depression from which I could not escape.

In the absence of any clinically approved solutions, I embarked on a dangerous course of self-medication. And although this was mainly facilitated by copious amounts of local cider, I would experiment with practically *any* substance that had the potential to relieve my depression. And virtually nothing was off the table.

My final Monkton Wyld term felt like the longest, saddest, Sunday evening sunset. Soon it would be a new day and a return to the realities of life back in London.

One by one, the people with whom I'd shared the bumpy ride into young adulthood began to drift away, and onto work, college or university. It was the end of an era, and for me, the end of freedom.

My final end-of-term school report stated:

*George (AKA Steven) has isolated himself from the rest of the school for much of this term. We hope his mood improves soon, and that he fulfils his dream of becoming a professional musician…*

## 26

# AFTER MONKTON

My First Job: August 1976

*Easytone Electronics* was situated on the Park Royal Industrial Estate, West London—a short train ride from home. It was a dismal place, devoid of nature and divided by a filthy canal where old men fished for any foolhardy creature brave enough to swim between the discarded shopping trolleys, and stagnant patches of oily residue.

*Easytone* were the manufacturers of ugly pink hearing aids that reminded me of deformed plastic prawns. And for the princely sum of sixteen pounds for a forty-hour week, my job was to fit each device with miniature amplifying circuit boards.

Whilst this was not exactly a prime position in the field of electronics, without qualifications or previous work experience, this was the best employment I could find. But it was also the type of soul destroying work that could drive even the hardiest of minds towards irreparable insanity.

In the staff canteen at lunchtime, I would sit alone and read whilst the long-term *Easytoners* ate their sandwiches in silence. They'd stare blankly into space as if watching an imaginary TV set—chewing on autopilot; expressionless, and resigned. No doubt wondering where their life had gone. Knowing that tomorrow would be exactly the same as yesterday, and next year will be identical to the one after. How long did it take for them to become like this I'd wonder? Eighteen-years? Five-years? Three-months? Was it even possible that such a state of catatonia may befall the less mentally stable in a single afternoon? Was I looking at who I may become if I stayed in that hellhole for another day? And was it true that after twenty-five years faithful service, *Easytone* retirees were rewarded with an attractive silver-plated carriage clock, and a free frontal lobotomy at the hospital of their choice? By the looks of things *some* workers had already opted for early retirement.

Please god—I'd pray whilst eating the tuna roll that tasted suspiciously like the previous day's chicken—don't let me become like one of *them.* Lead me out of this place before I lose the mental facility to quit…

September 1976 found London simmering in the afterburn of summer's slowly cooling furnace. Yet, still I yearned for Katy and my former life at Monkton Wyld. But time had moved on, and so had she. To Bristol, in fact, to live with her English mother.

I wanted to call her. To apologise. And to explain why I'd shouted at her in The Old Library earlier that year. But I didn't. I knew I'd struggle to get my words out and didn't think she'd want to talk to me anyway. So instead, I'd drink alone in my room after work each day and write songs about lost love and regret. The melodies would become sadder and sadder with each hopeless swallow. And the empty cans began to stack high on bedroom shelves like pointless monuments, where the things of my childhood once stood. This was a depression caused by *loss*, intensified by alienation, and prolonged by alcohol. I was trapped in a life I hated, and tormented by a past I could not change.

Autumn: 1976

When there are no earthly answers to life's insurmountable problems, people turn to religion and a host of other socially acceptable metaphysical beliefs.

But through the distortions of *my* tortured

madness, I concluded that desperate circumstances needed the type of dramatic solutions not found at the local synagogue on a Friday evening. And so, as the days darkened towards autumn, my thoughts turned towards the *Devil*.

My research led me to a store in Kensington where I purchased a copy of Anton LaVey's gloriously unholy work *The Satanic Bible*.

I devoured the book's alternative wisdom with my usual single-minded fervour, and for a while, was utterly convinced that the practise of *Black Magic* would, somehow, allow me to escape, to other less emotionally painful dimensions.

I had no evil intent, or any desire to hurt anyone. I simply didn't know how to cope with my depression, and thought that Satanism may provide the sanctuary other belief systems had not.

I'd visit the local park each night after work, and under the light of an autumn moon, would chant spells—hoping to be transported to a different reality. One in which I was back at Monkton Wyld with Katy.

To enhance the magic I bought an O*ris-root* pendant. This, I would dangle above a hand-drawn pentagram filled with strange mystical symbols. I'd sing songs about witches and fairies and midsummer nights in the forest.

Yet, despite my passion for the dark arts, I was not very good at the whole devil worshipping thing. For a start, I could not remember the long, wordy chants.

And squinting in the dark whilst holding a battery-powered torch to the Satanic Bible, spoiled the magic somehow. The spells were not working, and mum was growing increasingly suspicious about my nightly visits to the local park.

After a few months of unsuccessful devil worship, and without even the slightest whiff of an unnatural visitation, my faith in the little red-tailed guy and his big fiery promises began to wane.

Disillusioned, I put my well used copy of *The Satanic Bible* back on the bookshelf, and have not opened it since.

Now, I'm not necessarily suggesting that any of those spells cast in the local park had anything to do with it, but, shortly after my interest in Black Magic ended, and quite out of the blue, a letter arrived. It was from Katy. She was still living in Bristol with her mother and wanted me to visit her as soon as possible…

*Hi George, it would be great to see you again. My dad says he'll pay for you to come over to California with me—Love Katy x*

What did all of this mean? Why did she suddenly want me back? What would mum and dad say about me going to America? And what about my job wiring pink, plastic hearing aids, and my college course in TV maintenance?

So many questions, and so many thoughts to process. There was only *one* thing for it. At the first opportunity, I would travel to Bristol and speak to Katy in person.

A Few Weeks Later

With the uplifting melody of Peter Frampton's recent hit, *I want you... show me the way,* repeating endlessly in my head, I boarded the Bristol bound coach from London-Victoria. My hopes were high and my thoughts were only of Katy.

Some hours later I arrived in Bristol—anxious and expectant.

I had arranged to stay with my old Monkton Wyld musician friend *Mick,* who also lived in Bristol. Mick would show me around the town, and take me to the location where I'd meet Katy.

The following day, Katy and I were sitting in a Bristol, city centre pub. It was a rendezvous that was *not* go well—not that it was going *badly* either. Actually, it was a rendezvous that wasn't go *anywhere* at all. I'd managed to forget *everything* I'd wanted to tell her since my tragic faux pas at Monkton Wyld earlier that year. And any words that *did* escape from my frozen mouth, did so, in a kind of confused, clumsy stutter. And for the second time in six-months, my pathetic social skills had destroyed any chance of ever being with her.

It's not that I wanted to die, as such. It's just that I couldn't bare the pain of living any longer. I lay on Mick's bedroom floor with blood oozing from five gaping wrist wounds, and waited for the end. At my side lay a blunt razor blade—red-tipped and discarded. Praying that I had carved enough for nature to carry me to a less harsh place, I closed my eyes and let go into the darkness...

'*George*! Oh my god! What have you done?'

I opened my eyes to see Mick standing over me— wondering if I was dead.

'Bloody hell *George*, you were gone ages. I came upstairs to see if you were okay.'

Mick patched me up as best as he could with bandages from his mother's first aid box, but the wounds were deep and would need stitches. In the meantime, I had a train to catch, so hospital would have to wait until I got home the following morning.

Mick and I concluded that I'd probably passed out —*not* from blood loss—but from the afternoons reckless drinking, and the pills I'd found in his bathroom cabinet whilst looking for a razor blade.

'Sorry about your mum's carpet *Mick*, I didn't mean to mess it up. What will you tell her?'

'Never mind the bloody carpet *George*, you've really got to get over Katy. You can't carry on like this. Just focus on the thing you dreamt of at Monkton —becoming a professional musician.'

Waving goodbye to Mick, I boarded the late train to London, and prepared myself for the barrage of questions mum and dad would inevitably ask about the cuts, the blood, and the bandages.

* * *

Somehow, the suicide attempt in Bristol served to lance my toxic obsession with Katy. It may have been Mick urging me to forget her. Or perhaps the intensity of my feelings had simply run out of steam. Either way, I returned home from my disastrous trip knowing that if I didn't make some big changes soon, my next attempt to leave this world may be successful.

A few days later, and with my arms wrapped in clean, white bandages to protect the rows of unsightly stitches, I entered the Easytone building knowing I would not enter again.

The balding, bespectacled boss was sitting behind a desk piled high with paperwork, and prototype, pink, plastic prawns when I stormed in to his office and announced:

'This job is turning me into a cabbage. That's it! I've had enough! I quit!'

I slammed the Easytone door behind me and walked out into the mid-morning sunshine feeling empowered by my decision to leave. Now all I had to do was explain to my parents why I'd left a steady job with nothing else lined up to replace it.

## 27

# FUNK AND FINE FABRICS: 1978

*Musicians wanted. Must be funky and friendly. No time-wasters. Call Steve on 904-4692 for further information…*

Thus, read my advert in the back pages of *Melody Maker* in 1978.

For those too young to remember, Melody Maker was the weekly must-read for anyone seeking musical collaborators. For buying and selling instruments, and for catching up with the latest news from the world of rock music.

Nervously, I dropped the envelope containing my advert into the mouth of the postbox, and waited to hear it clatter down irretrievably into the unknown.

As it fell, I wondered how I would cope if anyone actually replied. Secretly, I wished my envelope would become lost forever in the bowels of Britain's monolithic postal system. Then I could say, *well, at least I tried, but it just wasn't meant to be…*

But, it *was* meant to be.

The following Thursday I stood in the tightly packed carriage of a rush hour tube train to read the following:

*Musicians wanted. Must be funky and friendly. No time-wasters. Call Steve on 904-4692 for further information…*


Goldbergs Fine Fabrics: 8:30 AM—1978

The carriage would have emptied and refilled at least three times by the time I got off at Bond Street Station.

I'd emerge up the escalator and onto a busy London pavement with Gerry Rafferty's *Baker Street* looping endlessly on my internal jukebox.

My destination is Goldberg's Fine Fabrics—a long-established store in the heart of the city's west end. My job is stockroom assistant, trainee sales-person and general crap-fetcher for the godawful Victoria Goldberg. And although my basement domain is something akin to a bleak Dickensian workhouse, the shelves are stacked full with the finest silk, cashmere, wool and cotton money can buy.

Initially, my role at Goldbergs was to keep the base-ment stockroom tidy, and to cut lengths of fabric as ordered by the sales staff upstairs. But within a year or so,

I'd morphed into a knowledgeable, if somewhat *nerdy,* fabric salesman—always on hand to advise customers on the advantages of *organza* over *chiffon*, *crepe georgette* over *challis*, and exactly how many yards of *Harris Tweed* are required to make a pleated, knee length skirt.

But one minute I was advising *Norman Hartnell* on fabric for the Queen Mother's new hat, or spending an entire morning with Kate Bush's costume designer, and the next, I was running errands for the horrendous Vikki Goldberg—bosses daughter and wannabe princess.

'Send the *boy,* (me) over to *Enrico's* to get a tuna-mayonnaise on brown,' she'd say—whilst applying multiple layers of industrial grade makeup to a sneering face.

*She'll need more than that to disguise such inner unpleasantness,* I'd think—briefly catching her reflection in the mirror as she barked even more insulting instructions…

'And tell the boy to pick up my dry-cleaning on the way back.'

Mr Taylor, the long-serving, super-submissive manager, would wink at me as if to say—*just ignore her Steve, it's not worth causing a fuss.*

But I wasn't like him, and so many times I almost lost control and said:

*Hey, Victoria, you've applied enough foundation on that spoilt face to build a skyscraper on top.*

Or:

*After you finish filling in the cracks, how about doing some actual work, instead of taking all the credit for mine?*

Sometimes, according to Vikki Goldberg, I was the *stupid boy*. The idiot incapable of returning from Enrico's with the correct lunch order...

'When is that stupid boy going to learn, I only have *one* sugar in my coffee?'

She'd growl loud enough for the customers to hear, as I handed her the wrong drink *again*.

'Someone tell him to go back to Enrico's and get two more coffee's—WHITE WITH WITH ONE SUGAR, AND ANOTHER ONE, BLACK, NO SUGAR'

By the time I'd reached Enrico's across the street, virtually all memory of the coffee order had vanished, and all I could do was make a hopeful stab getting it right.

For three, very long years, my imagination ran wild with ideas on how to exact my revenge on the delightful Ms Goldberg.

One night, I even had a dream in which some super strength LSD had fallen into her tub of low-fat, cottage-cheese, and she was dancing naked around the lamp-post in Bond Street announcing to the hordes of wealthy shoppers: '*I LOVE YOU CHARLES MANSON, I WANT YOUR BABIES...!*'

I awoke in a cold sweat—alarmed, yet strangely elated.

Somewhere in this multidimensional universe, Vikki Goldberg had finally received the humiliating justice she so richly deserved.

I'm not, by nature, a vindictive type of person who would ordinarily take delight in another's downfall, but as my Monkton Wyld school report once stated:

*George has an incredibly strong—if at times—blind sense of justice.*

I just like things to be fair, and for people to stick to the rules.

However, from my position of peak moral high ground, I am now prepared to cut Victoria Goldberg a large slice of historical slack. I shall assume that my karmic role in our relationship was to allow her to experience arrogance at the expense of my self-esteem. And to this end, my life's purpose is complete, and I am free.

I forgive you Vikki Goldberg—may your inner compass guide you to the land of low-fat cottage cheese and humility…

## Leroy: The Funkiest Bass Player In The World

I had just returned home from work when the phone rang:

'Hi is that Steve I'm calling about your advert in

Melody Maker. My name's Leroy and I'm the funkiest bass guitar player in London, *and* I've got some great contacts.'

This was my first ever conversation with someone of Jamaican heritage and I was immediately fascinated by the expressiveness of his English-Caribbean turn of phrase. Leroy's upbeat voice conveyed the wisdom of the street with the playfulness of a happy optimistic child. We spoke for a while and agreed to meet up on the weekend for a jam.

The following Sunday afternoon dad helped me lift my heavy guitar equipment into the back of his pristine black London taxi, and fifteen minutes later we arrived at the entrance of the notorious housing estate where Leroy and I had agreed to meet.

Almost immediately, dad and I were met by a short, but super-confident black guy sporting an impressive afro.

'Hi I'm Leroy,' he said cheerfully. We shook hands and exchanged a few awkward pleasantries. And soon, the unlikely cargo of oppressed minorities were heading deep into the heart of the troubled estate, where we were either going to play some funky music or get robbed of everything we owned.

Dad and I carried my equipment into a small, undecorated house that had, at some stage, become a rehearsal studio for local bands. The walls were lined with old mattresses to dampen the sound, and over the windows, carefully positioned blankets kept the secrets *in*, and the inquisitive eyes of local police *out*.

Most striking of all, however, was the dense cloud of something the inhabitants were calling *'erb*. It smelt familiar, but I knew it by a different name. but whatever this *'erb* thing was, it definitely added an interestingly heady ambience to the proceedings.

I later realised what 'erb meant and wondered how embarrassing it would have been if dad and I had been arrested in an unfortunately timed police drugs raid. What would mum have said? And what about the neighbours? They would not have forgotten the Monkton Wyld drugs raid scandal a few years earlier. Could the Slavins have survived a second lashing of local gossip?

Gradually the room began to fill with people—black people—all greeting each other with words I'd not heard before, and with elaborate handshakes I'd only seen attempted by *Huggy Be*ar in episodes of Starsky and Hutch.

Suddenly, the guy with a prominent gold tooth sat down at the drum kit and launched into a solid metronomic beat. Almost immediately the room burst into action. Leroy's powerful fingers slapped and pulled at his bass guitar's heavy strings, whilst others hit cowbells and shook tambourines. Then, as if standing on the edge of a swimming pool, summoning up the courage to jump in, I turned up the volume control on my black, electric guitar and I was *in*—strumming up and down with the same speedy rhythmic patterns I'd heard on the radio in the basement of *Goldbergs Fine Fabrics*

Leroy's smile was now wider than three Cheshire cats in a row. He was definitely *feeling the funk,* and so, evidently, was dad. He was in the corner of the room clapping along with impressive timing—just visible through a thick cloud of *'erb* smoke (not *his*, I hasten to add).

My fast, rhythmic guitar technique had pleased Leroy, and everyone else in the room gestured towards me whilst nodding in agreement. The general feeling was probably something like—*he may be white-ish, but he plays and sings like one of us.*

Before long, the room was jumping to the sound of wild afro funk rhythms, whilst exotic females whipped the air with colourful, beaded plaits—dancing and singing with wild abandon—the like of which I'd not seen before.

That afternoon I felt embraced and accepted—a part of something new and exciting. I had found my *tribe.* And by the end of my exhilarating baptism into the pulsating religion of *Black Music*, I was completely and utterly hooked.

Leroy knew everyone that mattered in the late 1970s British soul-funk scene. We quickly became friends, and within weeks of meeting him, I found myself at the centre of his exclusive social circle. Suddenly, I was on first name terms with musicians I'd only ever seen performing on TV. Everything was changing for me. There were new *rules* to learn and new fashions to embrace.

My new black friends dressed smartly. They went to night clubs where they danced with *girls*—instead of imaginary guitars. They drank rum and coke till the early hours, and always knew of a party where a hot plate of curry goat could be had for free on the way home.

For my nineteenth birthday, dad bought me a smart tweed jacket, and a pair of matching black trousers from Marks & Spencer. My hair was cut short by a trendy West-End stylist, and I would never leave the house without a quick squirt of Paco-Rabanne for men.

In 1979, the records that span on my turntable were by *The Average White Band, Chic*, and uplifting slices of musical mastery from *Earth Wind and Fire, and Stevie Wonder*. By day I was Victoria Goldberg's harassed dogsbody, and at night I was John Travolta in *Saturday Night Fever*—emulating Leroy's slick footwork across the floors of London's hippest venues.

Leroy was my friend, cohort and teacher. We'd talk for hours—he as wise mentor, and me, as naïve ex-boarding school boy, more used to the clucking of country chickens than the avoidance of inner city sharks posing as harmless dolphins.

He would delight in recalling his many conquests over the females of London: Black, white, Indian, Scandinavian, Irish—and often with a surprising amount of detail.

'Don't worry Steve, I'll get you *hooked-up.'* He'd say—flicking through the pages of his address book of likely candidates as though he could instantly command the presence of *any* female with a single phone call.

'It's okay, Leroy, I really don't want to be *hooked-up* thanks,' I'd reply—still in recovery from the trauma of losing Katy three years earlier. He'd smile, and close the little black book I was not allowed to examine. Perhaps the pages had been empty all along? This, I will never know.

Leroy was a hustler by necessity—super-cool and sharper than a diamond-tipped razor. He knew how to *play the game.* And to watch him slip and slide through life with barely the price of a train fare in his pocket, was a lesson in survival. Everywhere we went, Leroy seemed to *know* someone. He'd always get into nightclubs without paying, and once I even saw him put a coin into a bus drivers hand and retrieve it without the driver noticing.

Yet, despite being polar opposites, Leroy and I shared the same wild ambition. The dream of fame, fortune and multi-million selling records. All we needed to do was put a band together, and write a few songs that included the words—*get up, get on down, yowser,* and of course… *funk.*

## BOOM BOOM BOOM BOOM

Alvin, the drummer, kicks our newly formed funk band into action. Leroy's thumb slaps the strings on his bass guitar, and I play fast, rhythmic chords—strumming up and down like unrelenting mechanical pistons. Leroy nods his head towards the microphone stand and we burst into song:

'*Get up, get on down, get up, get on down, get up, get on down, get up, get on down.*'

I forget how many times we've sung, '*get up, get on down,*' and throw in an extra one just in case. Leroy gives me a hard stare, and I don't do it again.

The song Leroy has, somewhat predictably, decided to call *Get Up—Get On Down,* falls apart in an untidy fashion, and the guy hitting the cowbell appears *not* to have realised the song has ended. Leroy sucks his teeth and shouts at *Shirley*—one of our *two* Jamaican, female singers…

'You missed the *Get Up, Get On Down* before the third chorus.'

'NO, I NEVER!' Shirley fires back fearlessly.

'Look, Shirley, you may as well not be in the band. What's the point of rehearsing if you're going to get it wrong every time!' Leroy replies with equal scorn.

A huge argument ensues, and the attractive Shirley—dark skinned and slender—storms out with a decisive: 'Leroy... why are you such an *A-Hole?'*

Was this a question or a statement? I ponder as Alvin counts in the next song.

Leroy is now in a foul mood, and launches into another pounding baseline, which, to my ears, sounds virtually indistinguishable from the one on the previous song. We begin to sing:

'*We've got the funk, I've got the funk, you've got the funk, they've got the funk, he's got the funk, she's got the funk, who's got the funk? Everyone's got the funk.'*

Having confirmed for the thousandth time, that the entire human race was now in possession of that much sung about, yet undefined condition known as the *funk,* I couldn't help but wonder if the funk had also spread throughout the animal kingdom. Furthermore, boredom was driving me to speculate on whether hedgehogs, and goldfish, and Javan rhinoceri also get the funk? And what about dolphins and life forms that may exist on any—as yet—undiscovered distant galaxies? Did *they* receive any kind of mind-numbingly, banal interplanetary funk?

I, however, no longer had the *funk,* I had the cramp —and *badly*, in my left hand. It ached beyond words and was about to become a severe case of repetitive strain injury that may require surgery, and affect my entire career as a musician if I didn't stop strumming soon.

Midway through the song, my mind began to wander off again. Then, all of a sudden, I'd snap back into the moment and realise I'd been strumming away on autopilot for a scarily unknown number of bars. Much like driving along a fast, yet boring stretch of road for hours, when you suddenly realise you can't remember driving the previous mile. You ask yourself —*did I fall asleep...?*

Leroy shouts, '*CHORUS.*' I approach the microphone but forget the words, or, to be more precise, the correct order in which everyone received their funk. Was it *you? Me? Them? Everyone? No-one?* And do I really care? And is this even *music?* And when will I get a guitar solo? And just *how* exactly did I drift so far from my Monkton Wyld dream of becoming the next Eric Clapton or Neil Young…?

## 28

# HOWARD AND ME: 1980

*Question: What do you get if you cross an unachievable goal with a blind obsession?*

*Answer: Failure.*

In 1980, I became obsessed by the complex, spiritually tinged music played by those transcended masters of Jazz—*Miles Davis, Chick Corea and John Coltrane.*

Jazz was an art form that resonated well with my other new obsessions—*meditation,* and the search for meaning in realms beyond this harsh, physical world.

Following the disastrous ending to my relationship with Katy four-years earlier, I remained firmly of the opinion that interactions with the opposite sex were best left to the masochistically minded, and the socially adept—I was neither.

Those fleeting pleasures of life, the flesh, and the

egotistical quest for fame and fortune, were, I had decided, definitely *not* for me. Instead, I would become a Buddhist, and pursue a career as a musician in the niche world of Jazz.

Before long, my imagination was awash with intoxicating images just waiting to be realised.

Somehow, I was meditating on a warm stretch of golden sand to the sound of gently breaking waves. John Coltrane's soaring saxophone melody on his composition—*A Love Supreme*—would appear from nowhere like an orchestra in a Hollywood musical. Then, still in the full lotus position, a pose I could miraculously hold for days without suffering terminal cramp, I would strum rich, harmonious chords on my guitar to the song of soaring, white seagulls, squawking high in the blue beyond.

Back on planet earth, however, my worried father enquired, 'but how are you going to earn a living *Steven*... can you actually make any money playing *Jazz*...?' His forehead contorted into quizzical wrinkles, as he leaned out of the black, London taxi he was about to drive for the following fourteen-hours.

Dad had long conceded that a successful career in music was a realistic proposition for me. But Jazz... *really?* Surely there was no money in *Jazz*?

He was, of course, correct. There *was* no money in Jazz. Not unless your name was Miles Davis, or George Benson, or Herbie Hancock, or one of a handful of musicians whose brilliance, and luck, had taken them to the top of their genre.

How depressing it is to watch some talented, yet penniless old guy playing tired versions of Autumn Leaves and Summertime in *The Dog and Duck* on a Sunday afternoon? A lifetime spent learning all of those tricky Jazz scales—rewarded only by a free pint of warm beer in the back room of a half empty pub.

But aside from transcending Jazz's niche appeal, there was another reason I could not become a top flight Jazz musician, or, indeed, a top-flight *anything* that involved remembering things.

I am, of course referring to my great nemesis —*executive dysfunction.* That gigantic, ever-present, crapping elephant in the middle of every, single, bloody room I try to enter. I simply did not have sufficient mental capacity to remember all of those complicated chords, and altered scales commonly used in Jazz.

But still, I wasn't about to let a lack of brain power stop me from trying. So, when my guitar teacher *Richard* called to ask whether I would accept a short scholarship to study Jazz guitar at Goldsmiths University, I embraced the opportunity with open—if somewhat anxious—arms.

To my surprise, the course tutor was none other than the legendary American Jazz guitarist, *Howard Roberts.*

Howard was an old-school Jazz musician whose

long and distinguished career had begun in the 1950s. He once received the *Downbeat* award for best Jazz guitarist, and had played with all the greats: *Thelonious Monk*, *Peggy Lee, Milt Jackson* and *Art Pepper* —to name a few.

Howard still spoke in the Jazz *speak* of his youth. He said *cool* a lot, and called people *cats.* 'Man, those cats like *Miles* (*Davis*) were *far-out*…'

Howard was a man who'd been there and *done* it at a time in the evolution of Jazz, when people were *being* there and *doing* it for the very first time. He'd seen it *all* and wasn't about to take BS from anyone.

'Hey man… get your guitar out, let's play,' said Howard one afternoon, in a tone reminiscent of a 1960s black and white gangster movie.

*What!* The great Howard Roberts was asking *me* to *jam* with him?

So thrown was I by his request, I temporarily forgot how to open my guitar case.

'Breathe, man… *coool-out*,' suggested a chilled Howard. 'I watched you rehearse this morning, and you're playing was *far-out!'*

I took Howard's *hip* advice, and after a few deep breaths and a quick tune-up, we decided on *Autumn Leaves*—a tune I'd learned and forgotten at least a hundred times already that year. But I knew that with the grace of *God*, and a fair, far-out wind, I may just do enough to impress my hero.

'A-one, A-two, A-one two three four,' counted a

confident Howard, and we were *in*. I couldn't believe it! I was actually playing Autumn Leaves with *HOWARD ROBERTS*...

'Hey man, that's great,' remarked a visibly impressed Howard—who began altering the chords in the way that great Jazz players often do. And usually to an extent whereby the song becomes barely recognisable.

'Take a solo *man*, take a *solo!*' Demanded Howard from behind his fat, Gibson sunburst. And I obliged from behind my—not quite as fat—sunburst, George Benson style *Ibanez*.

Well, I don't quite know what happened that day, but I launched into one of the finest solos I'd ever played. My fingers seemed to glide with effortless precision to all the right places, *and,* at exactly the right time. It was like I'd been touched by the hand of God, or perhaps *Howard*—who's steady stream of 1960s buzz-words continued to accompany each and every one of my *far-out* notes...

'Hey brother, that's *hip.*'

And: *'Niiice.'*

And: '*Cooool man, cool.*'

And as that final *minor-ninth* chord with the *raised-fourth, flattened-fifth* and *deranged-seventh* rang out in the somewhat dissonant way that *Jazz* chords often do, Howard Roberts—the *coolest* daddy of the Jazz guitar—exclaimed just two words:

'*FAARRR-OUT…!*'

I leaned back in my chair with the inner satisfaction of a musician who would not require *any* further accolades to satisfy their ambition.

I, had jammed with the mighty Howard Roberts, and the mighty Howard Roberts had officially certified my playing as being, '*FAARRR-OUT…*' And that was enough for me.

If Howard had been even in the slightest bit concerned about this particular young cat stealing any of his well-deserved cream, he would not have had to worry for long.

The following afternoon, I attempted to blow Howard's mind for a second time in two days. This time with an ambitious version of John Coltrane's monumental composition *Giant Steps*.

In anticipation, Howard moved his chair a little closer, so he could observe my *far-outness* in even greater detail. But this time, all clarity would disappear under the heavy weight of a brain-fog's familiar veil . Nothing made sense, and my fingers felt as though they had been dipped in glue and left to harden overnight. It was an audio tragedy beyond redemption. I had been *found out* and wished I could turn the clock back to Howard's earlier perception that I was—very likely—the long-awaited reincarnation of *Wes Montgomery* (Google it!).

Howard winced, and shook his head slowly from side to side, as if to say: 'What the hell happened? I'm glad I'm not *you,* man.'

Howard's class ended for the day. And utterly deflated, I slammed the lid closed on my battered guitar case, and headed off across town to my nightly Jazz gig at *The Singapore Mandarin Restaurant* in swanky Holland Park.

On the final day of my scholarship I had a revelation. Even if, by some miracle, I ever became as good a guitarist as Howard—what would be the point? Was I really aspiring to be what *he* had already been in 1964? Perhaps Howard was simply one of the lucky few who'd hit the big time. There were probably thousands of Jazz guitarists as good as him, and I bet most of them were flipping burgers between gigs to make ends meet.

Suddenly, I could feel my previously unshakable passion for *Jazz* drain from every orifice. I did not want to be a failed Jazz musician, or indeed, a failed *anything*. And furthermore, I realised that my musical ambitions could not be contained within that tiny, under-the-radar niche called *Jazz*. I wanted more from life. I wanted excitement, money, and to live in a big house in the country—like the one John Lennon lived in when he sang *Imagine* to Yoko behind a white, grand-piano. I wanted rolling terraces, and a lake with swans, a yellow Ferrari, and a wall covered in multi-platinum discs confirming how *great* I was. But more than anything, I wanted to hear mum boast to Mrs White over the garden-fence…

'*Steven's doing just fine now. He's not abnormal any more. In fact, they say he's going to be bigger than The Beatles…!*'

Some time ago, I read that Howard had died at the tender age of ninety-two in his Seattle home. I have fond memories of the man who practically invented the word *cool*. And I expect that somewhere up *there* —high above the clouds in the big-blue-yonder— Howard will be happily jamming away on his fat Gibson sunburst with those other legendary *cats*: *Charlie Parker, Duke Ellington, Miles Davis*—and who knows, perhaps even the late, and very great *John Coltrane*.

## 29

## SORRY, I CAN'T REMEMBER

Studying Jazz at Goldsmiths had highlighted the sickening reality of my inability to remember things.

I may have been a pretty good guitarist, but—as is the case with the average *goldfish*—a memory can come and go in a matter of seconds. Only to be left for dead at the bottom of some murky cognitive pond.

But, to describe one's memory as being either *good* or *bad,* ignores the infinitely more nuanced way in which the brain processes information.

My autism diagnosis revealed that whilst my long-term memory is good, my short-term memory is not. My mental *log jam* happens at various stages of processing. The first of these blockages is my inability to understand what people are saying in the first place. Consequently, there is nothing to retain in memory other than the odd grasped word I attempt to reverse engineer into an approximation of the speaker's intended sentence. Most of the time I can get by in a conversation by nodding occasionally, and interjecting the odd comment that falls within the general scope of the discussion. This tactic has served me reasonably well over the years. But it does not work when I need to remember important information with any degree of accuracy. This is when I am *found out.* This is when the person talking to me is faced by a blank confused stare, and any previously held notions of my status as a responsible adult are quickly discarded.

My inability to process speech and language effectively, leaves me feeling isolated, stupid and unable to progress in life. This factor alone is enough to turn my autism into a disability, and every aspect of my life is affected. Whether I'm in a supermarket trying to remember how many cans of beans to buy, or standing on a stage in front of a thousand people with a guitar, an empty brain, and only the vague memory of a song I'd been rehearsing for weeks.

Many years ago, the band I was temporary a member of were booked to play a prestigious commercial gig on the *Isle of White*. For those not familiar with the British Isles, the Isle of White is a small picturesque island a few miles off the South Coast.

I boarded the band's coach in London, and a few

hours later was standing on the windy deck of a cross channel ferry looking out across the Solent's choppy waters.

I was looking forward to the gig that evening. We'd spent hours rehearsing the previous day, and as usual, I'd made doubly sure the song lyrics and chords were safely stored away in my guitar case.

With five minutes to go before the show was due to start, we scurried around like nervous rats on the darkened stage—making final adjustments to equipment, and carefully placing music charts on stands.

The electronic hum of powerful guitar amplifiers on standby was just audible above the packed crowd of wealthy clientele. And at the £500 per-head charity event, expectations for the evening's entertainment were high.

Suddenly the lighting guy throws the stage into spectacular brightness, the audience applauds and the drummer counts in the first song. It's the Marvin Gaye classic *Wherever I Lay My Hat*—a song I've sung many times over the years, but only with the aid of a clearly written song sheet.

BUT THEN DISASTER!

The dazzling white spotlights are switched to red —rendering the notation written on the paper completely invisible.

My immediate thought was: WHY, OH WHY, DID I CHOOSE TO WRITE IN *RED* INK WHEN I COULD SO EASILY HAVE USED BLUE OR

BLACK? But my brief analysis of which pen I should have used was quickly superseded by a far more pressing issue—*WHAT THE HELL WAS THAT FIRST CHORD!*

The song I'd learnt, but failed to retain any memory of a hundred times before, had begun and I needed to play *something*. I put my left hand on the fretboard and strummed a loud, confident *E Major*. My guess—although surprisingly *close*—was not quite close enough. The rest of the band were playing in *D*.

In perfect synchronicity, the entire front row of posh diners looked up from their prawn cocktails in shock at the sound of my deafening auditory clanger. And from behind me I could feel the combined hate-filled gaze of bass player, drummer, saxophonist and pianist.

But then things took a turn for the *even worse*. Not only had the red ink of the chord chart become invisible under the red, stage lighting, but also had the red ink of the song lyrics.

What was I going to do? I had to sing *something*. So I did what I'd always do when I'd forget the words —ad lib and hope the audience wouldn't notice.

For a while, I was getting away with it. The audience had refocused their attention to the generous portions of posh food and were quite oblivious to my lyrical misinterpretations. Until, that is, we got to the chorus. Then—as people often do when they recognise a familiar song—they begin to *mouth* the words. Unfortunately, their *correct* interpretation of *Wherever I Lay My Hat* did not correspond with my alternative version.

Once again, there were rows of men in evening suits, and women in glittery ball gowns looking up at the stage, and more specifically at *me*. Some looked puzzled—wondering if *they* were wrong or if it was *me*. Others simply chose to laugh. This, I found even more humiliating.

The song ended to muted applause. I stepped back from the microphone—shrugging my shoulders, and gesturing towards the lyric sheet that had just become visible again under a gentle blue spotlight.

The final insult to my injured ego came when a sozzled diner, who'd thought the whole thing had been particularly entertaining, called out, 'would you like *me* to sing the next one *mate*?' The rest of his table thought this was hilarious. I smiled and declined his sarcastic offer, whilst moving my music stand into the shadows—ready for the next song.

The perfect cognitive storm of auditory processing disorder and autism create a disheartening constant from which there is no escape. I cannot process what I cannot grasp, or remember that which slips through my memory the moment it enters. As a consequence,

I constantly relegate myself to the role of low functioning buffoon and leave the adults in the room to do all the clever stuff…

My wife Bonnie is preparing Sunday lunch. She tells me to open the cooker and to put the potatoes on the top shelf, the chicken on the middle, and to turn the temperature down to one hundred and thirty. I will, of course, do the complete opposite. Not because I wish to destroy the food, or my marriage, or cause a big argument. Far from it, I really hate conflict. It turns my stomach upside down and leaves me feeling upset for hours. It's just that my brain doesn't always work in the way I'd like it to.

The result will be squashy peas, cold, yet burned-to-a-cinder chicken, and nuked potatoes—blackened and barely recognisable.

The obligatory argument, focusing on my inability to do even the simplest of things, will ensue, and I'll disappear upstairs for an hour feeling like a complete moron. Meanwhile in the kitchen below, *Bonnie* restores life to a dinner that, for most chefs, would be beyond resuscitation. Communications are normally restored within twenty-four hours, followed by an uneasy peace that holds until another cognitive lapse ignites another drama.

So, whether it's destroying dinner, getting lost on roads I've driven down for more than thirty-years, or forgetting a song I've played a hundred times before, *executive dysfunction* is an autistic trait that frustrates me more than any other. It's the disability in my autism, and the impenetrable barrier that stifles my ambition.

Sometimes, the gift of *thinking differently* is simply not compensation enough…

## 30

### THE BEES: 1981

These were the days when the rawness of punk collided with Jamaican Ska music to become the New Wave urgency of bands like *The Police* and *The Specials.*

Leroy—my now, long-standing musical collaborator—and I, are standing side-by-side on a large, brightly lit stage perched high above the heads of a packed crowd.

It was the first London gig with our new band *THE BEES.* We are a six-piece multiracial, high octane, juggernaut. And the music we play is an aggressive hybrid of Funk, Punk, Rock, Ska and Reggae. We are loud, untamed and raw. An ambitious army of young musicians on a wild ride to an undefined *somewhere.*

Armed with guitars, saxophones, drums and keyboards, we strut like pre-fight boxers—assaulting the ear with all the energy and sneering arrogance our youth can muster.

The sea of hot colour in which I'm bathed alternates between red, blue, purple, green, and then red again. Either side of the stage, a mountain of black, sound equipment pummels an attentive audience into delighted submission.

This is what I'd always dreamed of. And for that short, yet magical forty-five-minute performance, every one of my teenage dreams of guitar-wielding greatness solidified into a brief moment of beautiful reality.

*THE BEES*—a name given to us by our manager —Eddie, are a diverse collection of souls whose paths would never have crossed if not unified by the drug of music.

Behind me on keyboards is *Damien* who'd just had a top ten record with his previous band *The Regents*, and would later introduce me to the late, great Chas Chandler—the man who discovered *Jimi Hendrix.*

At the back of the stage is *Errol* from Birmingham. A somewhat intimidating character, whose weapons of choice are drums, backing vocals and attitude.

Lead vocal duties are shared between *Frankie*, our blond David Bowie wannabe frontman, and the brown-skinned *Dawn*—girlfriend of Errol, and much needed eye-candy in an otherwise ragtag rogue's gallery of mismatched young men.

To my right, Leroy slaps his enormous bass guitar and sings the occasional backing vocal. He is more or less in charge of the band—lead hustler, the man that makes things *happen*. Leroy's other job is to shout a lot during rehearsals. This is mainly at Damien for being late, or at Dawn for singing the wrong words. This does not always go down well with boyfriend Errol who owns the exclusive rights on castigating his eye-catching other half.

Along with Leroy, I am the band's co-founder, guitarist and backing singer. *And*, as everyone kindly acknowledged, composer of the band's catchier songs.

At first, the gigs were small. I remember once playing to an audience that numbered less than the musicians on stage. At the end of each song, we were greeted by just three sets of applauding hands—the owner of the *fourth* set refusing to relinquish his grip on the pint of lager he'd been nursing for over an hour.

Those early gigs were like enhanced rehearsals—an opportunity to try out new songs and improve our stagecraft. But we worked hard, and with the help of prominent concert promoter *Marshall Arts,* we quickly gained a reputation as one of London's hottest new bands. For twenty-four exciting months, the venues grew larger, the audiences louder, and the distance between gigs further. And in everyone's opinion, the big time beckoned for the wildly ambitious BEES.

November: 1982

In 1982, the records playing on my stereo were by those soulful songsters: *Earth Wind and Fire, Randy Crawford* and *Heatwave*. So, when Leroy called to tell me *THE BEES* had been booked to open for the aforementioned *Heatwave,* I did what I always do when overwhelmed by information. I pace back and forth furiously, whilst waving my arms in the air as though attempting to fly and power-walk at the same time.

For those too young to remember, the original *Heatwave*—then in their prime—had scored an impressive number of international hits with: *Always and Forever, Mind Blowing Decisions, Boogie Nights* and *Gangsters of The Groove*. Meanwhile, co-founder Rod Temperton had gone on to work with *Michael Jackson* and *Quincy Jones* on The *Thriller* album. For the first time in my career, I felt as though I was in touching distance of a dream, and I could not believe my good fortune.

The back door of the band's truck opens, and finally, after hours of endless motorway, I extricate myself from the tiny pothole of a space between the piles of heavy sound equipment, and tumble out onto the road feeling sick, and disorientated.

We had arrived outside the theatre in Northampton just in time to see the members of *Heatwave*—dressed in classic 70s soul star attire—exit a small fleet of long, black limos.

Almost immediately, they are surrounded by a small group of giggling teenage girls chanting *HEAT-WAVE...! HEATWAVE...!*

They push through the crowd, signing a few autographs on the way, and disappear inside the theatre.

We unpack our gear, and an hour or so later, we take to the stage amidst a bustling crew of lighting riggers and equipment technicians for a quick soundcheck. We sound terrible—as though we'd never played together before.

Everyone is nervous and edgy, and an argument breaks out...

'WHAT THE F**K IS UP WITH YOU GUYS?' Leroy bellows angrily across the stage.

'WE'VE REHEARSED THIS SONG A THOUSAND TIMES AND YOU'RE STILL GETTING IT WRONG?'

Damien—scruffy, yet weirdly splendid in his

ripped *Rupert the Bear* trousers—fires back from behind his keyboards: 'F**k off Leroy, you're the one who came in at the wrong place…!'

Errol—from behind the dark shades, that were very likely surgically applied at birth—sucks his teeth loudly and hits a drum cymbal in anger.

*Dawn*—still ominously silent after an unresolved domestic with Errol the previous day—scowls with folded arms out into the empty arena from behind her squealing microphone.

I retreat to the back of the stage and pretend to tune up again—thus removing myself from all the unnecessary acrimony.

We return to the dressing room to put on our costumes, apply some space-age makeup, and mingle with the various members of *Heatwave.*

As 8:30 approaches, my stomach begins to churn in anticipation. Soon a stagehand will pop his head around the dressing room door and announce:

'Okay guy's…time to go on now—have a *good* one!'

*  *  *

'AND NOW… PUT YOUR HANDS TOGETHER FOR ONE OF THE HOTTEST NEW BANDS AROUND… THE BEEEES…!'

Temporarily leaving all the bad feeling in the

dressing room, we run out onto the stage and into a familiar blast of heat and colour.

*ONE TWO THREE FOUR* counts the unflappable Errol from behind his drum kit, and suddenly THE BEES explode into loud, post-punk musical anarchy —not at all what the soul-loving crowd expected of a Heatwave—supporting band with *black* people in it.

I wave to my sister and her friends a few rows back in the audience, and turn to smile at Leroy—just in time to see his heavy bass guitar hit the floor, and bounce with a heart-stopping raspy-thump, before coming to rest in the glow of an orange spotlight.

On Leroy's left shoulder are the threadbare remains of a frayed guitar strap—no longer able to support the weight of his hefty instrument.

Never being one to shirk my responsibilities when staring down the barrel of a loaded *Heatwave* audience, I instinctively leap across the stage to help Leroy lift the heavy bass guitar, and return it to the safety of his sweaty arms.

Meanwhile, the band play on—albeit bereft of pounding bass, and funky guitar rhythm.

Leroy leaves the stage for what seems like an eternity, and returns with a spare guitar strap just in time for the final chord.

The song ends, and to my surprise, the audience reward our embarrassing antics with some unexpectedly enthusiastic applause.

But *why*? I wondered, would anyone applaud such

unprofessionalism? Surely everyone must have seen Leroy's bass guitar crash to the ground, *and* my spectacular dive across the stage to rescue it?

After the show, my sister and her friends came backstage to meet the band.

I was still embarrassed about the mishap on our opening number. But when I mentioned the incident to her, she replied, 'oh, I thought that was just part of your act… wasn't that *supposed* to happen?!'

Now I knew why the audience had applauded so enthusiastically. They must have thought we were some kind of musical-comedy act! One that combined old-school slapstick, with edgy, high-octane funk. *We could be on to something here,* I considered for a second or two, before quickly dismissing the idea as stupid.

## Life In The Fast Lane

Just when I thought the strange well of unintended drama had been exhausted, the universe thrust one final act into my evening of unimaginable weirdness.

I decided to travel back to London in my sister's car—thus, avoiding another hair-raising journey squashed into the back of the band's truck.

There were five of us in my sister's sporty little *Morris Coupe*. I drove whilst she napped soundly on the front passenger seat. In the back, her three friends sat silently—probably still wondering how long it had taken us to perfect the ingenious, *broken-bass-guitar-strap* routine.

Suddenly there was a loud bang and our car plummeted sideways across all three lanes of fast-flowing motorway traffic. Our tyres screeched and squealed as we slammed violently into the central barrier separating us from the deadly rush of oncoming traffic.

Again and again we lurched—spinning and rebounding off the crash barrier before coming to a halt on the muddy, grass verge.

Then there was silence. Just the ratcheted-clicks of *me* pulling up the handbrake as if honouring the memory of Mr Barnham—my old driving instructor.

'Never forget to apply the handbrake when stationary,' he'd say—so I always did.

Somehow, I pushed open the mangled door and climbed out. Both tyres on the driver's side had disintegrated, leaving hot, metal-discs steaming and wedged firmly into the wet mud.

On the far side of the road, the car that caused the accident had come to a halt on the hard shoulder. Its male driver lay semi-conscious on the cold tarmac. We later found out he'd fallen asleep at the wheel, and had slammed into the back of us at seventy-miles-per-hour.

Soon there were sirens, and the blue flashing lights of police cars and ambulances—spectacular against the black, 2 am sky.

We stood by the side of the road wondering what

to do next, when, from nowhere, a long black limo slowed to a stop alongside us. It was *Heatwave* returning to London from the gig!

The electric window at the back descends with the effortless cool of a sweet, soulful ballad, and a deep American voice asks, 'hey, are you guys ok?'

Still dressed in the sparkly stage outfit, and David Bowie inspired makeup I'd forgotten to remove, I reply, 'yes, Keith *(*Wilder*)* thanks... we're fine.'

The limo's electric window rose to a shiny black tint, and *Heatwave* glided casually away into the darkness, like a luxury ocean-going cruiser destined for sunnier climes.

Some months later I received £500 compensation for the whiplash injuries I suffered to my neck. I used the money to buy a brand new guitar—a beautiful sunburst *Ibanez,* that enabled me to earn a living for a good number of years.

It's like they say in America—when life hand's you lemons, make lemonade. So I did.

After two years of non-stop gigging, the *nearly-made-it BEES* came to the end of the road.

Gradually, the big halls became the backroom of a pub somewhere in East London. And the small crowd of screaming teenage girls that once chased Frankie and I along Battersea High Street in search of an autograph, had deserted us in favour of those genuine eighties pop stars—*Duran Duran*, and *Spandau Ballet.*

Without a record deal in sight, THE BEES staggered to their inevitable demise. Just as well really. It was only a matter of time before someone would have been killed during a typically bad tempered rehearsal. Probably by a low-flying amplifier, or carefully aimed drumstick.

It's always better to quit over musical differences than to face a lengthy prison sentence for murdering the drummer because he was late for rehearsals —*again*.

Our final gig was at an air force base in Yorkshire. It was a disaster. Errol and Dawn pulled out at the last minute—leaving a member of the road crew to stand in on drums, and me to sing all of Dawn's high, girly parts. 'Who's the *bird with the moustache?'* A member our esteemed Royal Air Force was heard to enquire loudly, whenever I did my high-pitched Dawn impersonations. It must have looked, and sounded ridiculous. Nonetheless, Leroy and I tried desperately to resuscitate the dying spirit of THE BEES one final time, but it was no good. The gig was little more than a weary, inauspicious swansong for a band that had once flirted with the big time.

## 31

# THE STRANGEST LOVE OF ALL: 1982

The first time I saw *Molly* was in 1982 at the super-trendy Camden Palace. She was a mixed-race beauty with wild hair and strange clothes—a girl who knew *everyone* that mattered on the London club scene.

Molly would enter a club, and within seconds, be surrounded and swept away into a crowd of adoring men, fabulous women, and flamboyant transvestites.

Slender, coffee-skinned and topped by a mass of dark, cork-screw hair, one's first impression of her was always, '*WOW!*'

Leroy and I would often bump into Molly at clubs around town. He would always joke about how he could *have* her if he put his mind to it. I'd say nothing, knowing that she was probably way out of his league.

Leroy and I would spend a good deal of time discussing Molly. And in the cold light of day would agree that *looks* weren't everything. And besides, all she does is talk about herself.

Indeed, a conversation with Molly was not unlike a quick-fire press release given on behalf of a wannabe celebrity.

In one long sentence, I'd be informed of her burgeoning modelling career, and an update on all the famous people she'd met that week, and just how incredibly wonderful they'd all thought she was. And then she was gone—lost to the beckoning calls of, MOLLY...! HI...!DARLING...! YOU LOOK DEVINE , LET ME BUY YOU A DRINK...!

Leroy would laugh and say, 'are you sure you don't want me to *fix* you up with her Steve? In fact Leroy had been saying he'd *fix* me up for years, but by all accounts he wasn't doing such a great job of fixing *himself* up! Not if his recent attempts at flirting with Molly were anything to go by.

The previous week I'd heard her remark loudly, at a social gathering: 'LOOK, LEROY, YOU'RE WASTING YOUR TIME, I DON'T FANCY YOU, AND I DON'T DATE BLACK MEN...!

And when it later emerged that Molly's preference was, in fact, for Jewish men with long wavy hair, Leroy finally conceded that, she wasn't *his* type anyway, and was only pretending to fancy her for a laugh!

\* \* \*

Anyhow, as fate would have it, and to everyones utter astonishment, Molly and I found ourselves in a relationship that no-one could have predicted, and many warned would end badly.

## Our First Date

Molly had invited me to watch her strut the catwalk during *London Fashion Week* at London's Kensington Olympia. Her modelling partner was none other than *Sade*—a year or so before she'd hit the big time. After endless rounds of that double-cheek-air-kissing thing I find so embarrassing, *and* more than a little unhygienic, Molly and I drove further into town for yet more double-cheek-air-kissing, in the places frequented by the good and the great of London's underground elite.

An hour or so later, we were downstairs at *Candy's—a* trendy basement bar near Piccadilly. Joining Molly and I, at the cosy little table for four were *Janice*—a large man in a cream wedding dress, and the influential *Philip Sallon.* Philip was less formally dressed than Janice—choosing a simple red and yellow clown outfit with bowler hat and matching bow tie.

As a quick aside, Philip was one of the great movers and shakers of his generation—a key architect of the London club and fashion scene. Molly was one of his *in-crowd*, and so, by default, and despite my

*ordinary* clothes, and Italian waiter style moustache
—was I.

Anyhow, lets recap:

It's my first date with Molly, who, after a few
drinks could not decide on whether she was *Grace
Jones*, *Diana Ross* or *Stevie Wonder* (more on this
later). Opposite me sat the six-foot-something *Janice,*
who's grisly twelve o'clock shadow was just visible
through the veil of his elaborate, cream coloured,
wedding dress. And next to *Janice* sat *Philip Sallon,*
in a red and yellow clown suit.

I hardly said a word, I felt *so* out of place and
uncomfortable in my ordinary jeans, ordinary shoes
and ordinary T-shirt. In fact, I was the exact picture of
high street averageness these titans of New Romantic
fashion were rebelling against.

Then, suddenly, above the noisy hubbub of pretty
young things, came a loud and familiar voice:

*'MOLLY...! HI... DARLING...! YOU LOOK
DIVINE...! LET ME BUY YOU A DRINK...!'*

With this, Molly and Philip both stood up and
adjourned to another table to mingle with their *divine*
admirers. Now it was just me and Janice. The oddest
of odd couples. Janice looked as uncomfortable as I
felt, but at least he made the effort to engage me in
some awkward small talk. Through a small opening in
his lacy head dress, the pre-bearded Janice enquired,
in a voice deeper than I'd expected:

'So, Steve, do you come here often?'

'Err, no, actually it's my first time. How about *you*... Janice? Do *you* come here often?' I replied, desperately trying to keep the *do you come here often* conversation going until Molly returned to save me. But then, in a moment of extreme social panic I jumped out of my seat and bolted for the men's toilet door, leaving Janice to drink alone.

Overcome by anxiety, I remained in there for a good hour, trying not to give the impression I was hanging out in the mens bathroom for reasons akin to the steady flow of male visitors dressed as belly dancers, geisha girls and ballerina's—each one emptying their bladder of cheap red wine before filling their nostrils with suspicious white powder.

Finally, Molly returned to the table, and I gained enough confidence to leave my insalubrious hideaway to join her.

On the way home, she delighted in telling me how her friends had asked *why* she was dating such an ordinarily dressed guy? 'It must be his personality!' Appeared to be the overall consensus. I did not reply, and spent the rest of the journey feeling just a little bit smug that perhaps it really *was* because of my, 'personality,' that Molly had chosen to be with me.


Date Number 2

Sade—friend of Molly's, and soon to be international singing superstar—invites the two of us along to

*Ronnie Scott's* in Soho. And along with a small handful of press and record company executives, we watch her band *Pride* perform a short showcase.

The band begins to play, and the spotlight falls on *Sade*. She is extraordinary—not like the Sade I'd seen backstage when modelling with Molly. She is exquisite, statuesque and intoxicating. I turn to Molly and say, 'Sade's amazing, but she'd be better off without that band behind her!' Molly agrees.

We didn't see much of Sade after that night at *Ronnie Scott's*. And a few years later, I watched her on TV performing *Your Love is King* in front of millions at Live Aid. I always knew that girl was special, I thought—wondering if she'd remember me if I ever bumped into her again...

I'd felt for some time there was something strangely dark about Molly. Something I couldn't quite put my finger on. But whenever I'd visit her in that spooky old house on the hill, I'd always look forward to 10 pm when it was time to leave. Her irritable Irish mother would bang on the bedroom door and shout…

'Tell that boy he has to go *now* Molly, it's not right, it's just not right…'

I'd be up and out of Molly's house like a hare from a starting gate, and in my red Morris Marina, locking its rusty doors faster than a champion speed-reader could spell *Amityville horror.*

During the course of an evening, Molly's personality could switch, in an instant, between the calm normality of the *nice* Molly, into a version that was wholly detached from reality—spiteful and devoid of empathy. *This* version Molly scared the living hell out of me. And during the eighteen months we were together, other versions of Molly began to appear. It was like dating at least three different people, and in all honesty, I couldn't decide which one I liked the least.

Once we were in a pub following a fashion show at the famous *Central Saint Martin's College of Art.*

Molly, over-excited by her catwalk triumph that afternoon, became a version of herself even *I* hadn't seen before. After a drink or two she completely lost control and was up, dancing on the tables and singing Diana Ross songs at the top of her voice. By the time the police had arrived to take her, and the other female models away, the otherwise sedate pub had erupted into something akin to a wild west saloon style brawl. Tables were overturned, and beer mugs were sent flying through the air—as were an impressive collection of designer shoes and other fashionable clothes.

For a while, the police presence served only to intensify the chaos. But eventually the officers seized control and hauled the over excited models out onto the street, still kicking and screaming.

Powerless to do anything, I stood well back and looked on in horror as Molly—now in floods of tears, having whacked a policewoman in the face—was led away in handcuffs. 'DON'T JUST STAND THERE YOU IDIOT, DO SOMETHING!' She screamed at me, as two burly policemen dumped her unceremoniously in the back of the van, before slamming the door and driving off at speed.

The beer-sodden floor was left strewn with the colourful contents of make-up bags, pink and purple wigs, and gold lame dresses.

I stood quietly amongst the wreckage of the pub, trying to understand what had just happened, and what it was that had provoked Molly to morph into some kind of deranged Dianna Ross.

I apologised to the pub's manager, and left—scooping up as much abandoned modelling paraphernalia as I could on the way.

Molly was finally released at around 6 am after a night in the cell. We had some breakfast, and made our way to the court where she was fined for assaulting a police officer, and being drunk and disorderly.

I was angry with her for causing such an unnecessary incident. But on the drive home, my anger turned to sadness and concern.

'The ghosts… they come into my room *every*

night. They shout at me, and won't let me sleep,' explained Molly, as the windscreen wipers pushed the greasy London drizzle from our view.

She told me how her strict, Irish Catholic mother had been so ashamed of having a child with a black man, that no one back home in Ireland even knew she existed. And how her mother would never sit next to her on the bus, or walk along the street holding her hand—fearful of being associated with a mixed-race daughter. And as a child—Molly was sent away to a convent school where the nuns would beat her, and call her a *black bitch.*

Then I remembered the previous Easter, when her mother had invited me over for Sunday lunch. We ate roast chicken and potatoes around a small, rickety table in the middle of a dimly lit kitchen—and tried to think of things to say:

'Lived here *long, Mrs…* err, sorry, I mean *Miss…* umm…?' Realising that I didn't *actually* know her name.

Molly had a long, and very complicated Nigerian surname, and had only ever referred to her mum as the *silly old cow next door*—I couldn't really call her *that.* And just when I thought the situation couldn't get anymore awkward, Molly's mum suddenly went on the attack in her god-fearing Irish accent:

'SO… YOU, YOU KILLED OUR LORD…!'

'What, *me…?'* I replied, wondering if, perhaps, I'd misheard what she'd said.

'YES, YOU… YOU JEWS… YOU KILLED OUR LORD. YOU'LL BURN IN HELL YOU KNOW…!'

Molly threw her head back as far as it would go— a bit like that scene in the *Exorcist*—and begins to laugh hysterically.

'OH, SHUT UP MUM, YOU SILLY OLD COW… *YOU'RE* THE ONE THAT'S GOING TO BURN IN HELL…!'

* * *

A few weeks after the pub incident, I dropped Molly home after an evening at Ronnie Scott's club. She'd been acting strange all evening—throwing money all over the place and claiming she was Diana Ross.

Somewhere around 2 am I pulled up outside her house. I was tired, and stressed out, and just wanted her to get out of the car so I could be alone.

'Goodnight *Moll,* I'll call you tomorrow,' I said— turning to kiss her on the forehead. Suddenly her eyes appeared to pop out of her head—white, and widened in abject fear. I recoiled back in my seat. This was not Molly any more—at least not any of the Molly's I'd previously known, and, in a voice that was manic, other-worldly, and quite unattached to all she had been before, she began to sing…

*'STOP IN THE NAME OF LOVE, BEFORE YOU BREAK MY HEART.'*

'DID YOU KNOW I'M DIANA ROSS...?' She screamed at me. 'NO, I MEAN MICHAEL JACKSON—YES, I'M STEVIE WONDER—MY *CHERIE AMOUR, LOVELY AS A SUMMER'S DAY.'*

Molly was laughing, crying, and laughing again—the car rocking side to side by the force of her ungodly agitation. 'YOU'RE THE DEVIL, YOUR JESUS, YOU'RE THE DEVIL, YOUR JESUS,' she screamed at me from the front passenger seat, and through a mass of wild corkscrew hair...

4 am

Molly and I are in the emergency ward of a North London Hospital. She's calm but terrified.

The psychiatrist says, 'hello Molly—come back to see us again have we?'

'What? You've been here before?' I ask.

Molly nods, and replies. 'Yes, in the *funny-farm...'*

'You haven't been taking your medication have you Molly?' The doctor asks as if scolding a naughty child.

'It's best you leave this to us now *Steve*, she'll need sedating. Go home and get some rest.'

'NO, PLEASE DON'T LEAVE ME HERE, I'M *SO* SCARED, I'LL BE GOOD... I PROMISE...' Molly cries from the depth of her soul.

The doctor looks at me and gestures towards the

exit. I leave her, and feel every ounce of pain mum must have felt at the end of visiting time when I was a child in Great Ormond Street Hospital, begging to go home.

I'd not seen anyone as desperate and broken as Molly that night, but I had to leave her in the care of the doctors, there was really nothing else I could do.

I arrived home around 8 am that traumatic Sunday morning and crawled into bed—exhausted, yet unable to sleep. Sometime later, mum brought me up a soothing cup of hot tea. 'Is everything all right dear?' She asks.

'It's Molly,' I replied. 'I had to take her to the hospital, she's not very well. I don't think we'll be getting engaged after all.'

It seems that no one is immune from mental illness. Not even gorgeous, cutting edge fashionistas with Diana Ross hair, and friends in high places.

I have no idea where Molly is now, but I truly hope that somehow, she eventually found peace…

# 32

## AD2000: 1982

Leroy and I are in a Camden recording studio with our new band *AD2000*. We have a record deal with *Polydor* in Germany, and another with *Red Bus* in the UK. With the addition of ex-Hi Tension guitarist (and future best-man) *Paul*, we're busy laying down the rhythm section for the first single. Dave from *Sade's* band puts down a great drum track, whilst Leroy and I add some *funky* bass and guitar.

I remember Paul saying something about, 'some girls,' coming down later to sing backing vocals, but after two sleepless days and nights in the studio, I was too tired to take much notice of this comment.

Later That Day...

Paul, Leroy and I are standing behind the mixing desk

staring out into the recording area through the glass partition window.

Three women, one black, one Asian and another, of mixed race appearance, are singing into a large studio microphone. Immediately, my eyes are transfixed on the mixed-race girl in the checkered shirt. She's stunning, visually, but also spirited and funny, and not afraid to speak her mind when necessary—something *I'd* always wished I could do.

Her name was *Bonnie*, and in between vocal takes, we began to chat over late night cups of studio tea. And although our backgrounds were worlds apart, we seemed to hit it off pretty well.

The session ended as the dawn began to light the Camden sky. I dropped her home to nearby Islington and headed off home for some much needed sleep.

All I could think about on that early morning drive home, and, indeed, for the following few days was *Bonnie*. I wanted to see her again. But for now, the exotic girl in the checkered shirt would remain a distant, impossible dream.

Some Months Later...

All six members of AD2000—including Bonnie and I —are touring the UK clubs promoting our first, and then our second singles.

Unlike *THE BEES*, AD2000 do not play *live*. We do not take to the stage with guitars, drums and keyboards. Instead, we are a vocal group that dances and mimes. And when the song finishes we throw free copies of our record to the outstretched arms of a grabbing audience.

I, however, cannot dance. I'd do my best on a night out with Leroy, but my limbs have a way of dancing independently of each other, and only occasionally cross paths in what could vaguely be described as synchronicity.

After a number of pointless–*how to walk in a straight line without falling over*—lessons failed to improve things, I was duly relegated to studio *only* duties. I hate to fail at anything, but in this instance, I was more than happy to accept my demotion.

This was *not* before I'd already taken to a hundred different stages dressed like early incarnations of Boy George: hair and make-up courtesy of Molly—alternative fashionista, and soon to be ex-girlfriend.

Soon, both Molly *and* AD2000 would have come and gone, and I would move on to growing my relationship with Bonnie, whilst pursuing a solo career in music.

I often wonder how our lives would be if everything we hoped to achieve came to fruition? Would we swap our intended goals for our present circumstances?

Probably not, but sometimes it's fun to play the *what if game*.

What if THE BEES *had* reached the heights

everyone had predicted? And what if AD2000 *had* become a worldwide smash? What if Leroy had not seen my *musicians wanted* advert in Melody Maker years earlier. And what if Leroy hadn't introduced me to Paul, who'd introduce me to Bonnie...?

Could it be that everything is preordained? Or are the circumstances in which we find ourselves shaped by nothing other than chance?

In reality, we have little choice other than to work our way through action and consequence—blinkered, and constantly changed by the unforeseen. We enter the maze at birth hopeful that, one day, our exit will open into a vast expanse of riches. But as the years go by, we realize the maze *has* no exit—only stop off points along the way where we may rest occasionally with our temporary gold.

As the saying goes, there is no such thing as a rich man in a cemetery…

## 33

BONNIE: 1984

For the record, I would like to state that no one has supported, and believed in me more than my wife of over thirty-years *Bonnie*.

I would also add that no one has suffered more at the hands of my social ineptitude than her.

Speak to any woman with an autistic husband or partner, and you'll find striking similarities in their testimony.

Women talk about nights spent alone whilst their autistic husband locks himself away in another room —indulging in some obsession or another.

They talk about a sense of separateness, and feeling lonely even though they are not *alone*. They say their autistic husbands are emotionless, and rarely display affection. And in almost every case, women say its like living with a child. They organise his day, his clothes, his meals, his finances, the kids, the holidays, the shopping, Christmas, birthdays. It's as though they were their husband's mother, father, accountant, cook, cleaner, carer, travel agent and car mechanic.

Neurotypical women speak about how their autistic husband is unable to see *their* point of view, and about the constant arguing over wrongly interpreted remarks.

Is it any wonder that so many women in this position say that although they love their partners, they have become utterly exhausted by the daily struggle to keep the relationship alive?

It's into the context of this preamble, that I introduce *Bonnie*—the woman who dragged an immature twenty-three-old man-child kicking and screaming into a vague semblance of adulthood.

Bonnie is the beautiful daughter of a Nigerian father, and a white English mother. She is a straight-talking North London girl—independent, super-smart, and quite a catch for an autistic, guitar playing ex-hippie like me.

'Could have been a doctor–*that* one,' dad always says of his exotic daughter-in-law's academic potential.

'Perhaps a psychologist would have been more useful in the circumstances,' I jokingly reply, whilst stopping for a second to consider *just* how useful this could have actually been.

Another thing I've always admired about Bonnie is her honesty. Her philosophy is simple…

'If you don't want to hear what I *really* think, then don't ask me the question.'

And whilst, given the choice, we'd opt for the soft landing of an answer that would comfort our self-delusion, we are always likely to learn more about ourselves from the hard reflection of uncomfortable truth—especially when this truth is delivered by a close friend.

And regardless of what may be said during the impassioned heat of battle, Bonnie will *always,* and without condition, be my closest and dearest friend.

## Before My Autism Diagnosis

'I've always thought you were, sort of… well, emotionally cold and detached.'

I drift off into thought—not knowing how to respond.

'I mean it!' Bonnie repeats. 'I *really* think you come across as emotionally cold and detached.'

Again, I drift off into deep, extended thought—carefully assessing the implications of her comments.

'SEE?! That's *exactly* what I mean…Have you *not* got anything more to say about the fact I've just called you *emotionally cold and detached?'*

She breathes a heavy, exasperated sigh and I snap back into the conversation's harsh reality.

'Ah, yes,' I reply.

'About being *emotionally cold and detached*—can I get back to you on that…?'

And I will, someday. Just as soon as I figure out exactly what she means by *emotionally cold and detached*.

Bonnie goes to bed justifiably frustrated, and I'm left feeling confused, and I don't know how to put things *right*. I make her some tea, by way of a peace offering, and take my evening *Zoloft*—pausing briefly before swallowing to thank the little white pill for keeping me calm in the face of adversity.

I open my notebook and write on the following day's to-do list:

*Speak to doctor about upping the dose...*

'The problem *is,*' I explain to Bonnie sometime later, 'I just can't seem to work out what people *really* mean.'

I do my best to describe the type of social dyslexia people like me struggle with—but it's hopeless. A bit like describing the colour *blue* to someone that has only ever seen *yellow*. I cannot blame her for not understanding how I see the world. After all, none of us can truly understand another's lived experience.

Bonnie would have also been wholly justified in assuming my baffling strangeness was little more than the supreme selfishness of an obsessive, career-driven narcissist, intent on achieving success—regardless of the consequences. The greatest gift afforded by my autism diagnosis in 2008, was a small crack of light with which we could begin to examine the motivations behind my often problematic approach to life.

I shall end this chapter by saying that whilst Bonnie may never become an expert in the field of autism, she is doing her absolute best to become an expert in the field of *me*. And for this alone, I thank her.

## 34

### FINDING MY IDENTITY

I did not learn to socialise in the normal way. As a child my world was small and turned inwards. My *friends* lived inside the little black and white TV set in the corner of the lounge. Other friends lived in toy boxes piled high at the end of the bed. My inanimate roommates were made of plastic and wood, and metal, and had identical nondescript expressions carved into their tiny faces.

My fear of engaging with anything beyond the garden gate, had driven me towards complete social isolation. And in the absence of *human* friends, I adopted the speech and behavioural patterns of my favourite TV superheroes. Saturday morning viewing began with *Thunderbirds*. Someday, I too would save humanity from a gigantic asteroid hurtling towards the earth at the speed of sound.

Then I was *Batman*, and I was also *Robin*. From

these heroic, caped crusaders I discovered justice and morality, and how to combine violence with camply delivered punchlines. Their paper thin personalities gave me a frame of social reference devoid of the slightest ambiguity. As far as our dynamic duo were concerned, people were either good, or they were *very* bad, and the very *bad* ones must be defeated...

'Holy crab cakes *Steven,*' a colourfully costumed *Robin* would exclaim. 'What are we going to do now?!' In response, I'd leap onto the sofa and give one of mum's plump, flowery cushions a thoroughly good beating.

'Holy crushed velvet *Steven*! Those evil soft furnishings won't be troubling *us* again...!'

I entered adolescence as a patchwork quilt of borrowed beliefs and copied vocabulary. To the neighbours, I was still the dysfunctional child who'd been sent to a *special* school in the countryside. And at seventeen, I added to this perception by being the only boy in Grasmere Avenue with crazy hair, crazy ideas, and a mode of speech that all too often created a look of confusion on people's faces.


In 1977...

Having spent the previous year studying Shakespeare's *Richard III,* I decided to adopt the 16th century linguistic style of the great bard, until a more suitable mode of speech came along...

*'Would thou, kind sir, bestow upon me a cup of your noble beverage…?'*

I once enquired when ordering a white coffee in a West End cafe. Confronted by a confused barista, and an irritable lunchtime queue building up behind me, I bowed to the social norm and reverted to current vernacular: *'Coffee please mate—one sugar!'*

In 1978…

Following a short spell working on a friend's farm in Dorset, I mysteriously developed a West Country accent so strong that it tipped over into a kind of strange Irish twang.

I remember someone asking:

'Are you *oyrish*?'

'No,' I replied, *'oim frarm Daarzet.'*

*'*Sounds *loik oyrish* to me,' said the man from Belfast with a disbelieving look on his face.

My search for identity continued unabated.

In 1979…

I thought my friend *Leroy*—bass guitarist and mentor —was the coolest black dude in town, and, of course, in my imagination, so was *I*.

The mirror said otherwise. As did my distinct lack of dance-floor dexterity.

In 1980...

I was briefly, a character from the hit film *Fame*. I was the male equivalent of the streetwise, quick-witted, New York dance student *Coco Hernandez*.

'*Ya gadda do, wat ya gadda do to get orrn in this world—no-*ones *gonna do it forrr* ya!' I once explained to my mother. 'Yes, son, that's right, but *why* the American accent…?'

In 1982...

I had another go at being *black*:

The phone rang, it was *Dawn*—singer with my band *THE BEES,* and girlfriend of *Errol*—also a member of *THE BEES*.

She—the subject of an intense crush.

He—six-feet tall and impressively muscle-bound.

'Hi Steve, it's *Dawn*. What time are we rehearsing today?' She asked in a soft, husky tone that left me wondering if she really meant something *else*.

'Hi Dawn,' I answered in an *Errol* tinted voice so deep I could almost see the glass vibrate in my bedroom window.

'Is this your *new* voice?' She enquired with a hint of amusement.

Immediately, I was overcome with embarrass-ment. How could she have known I was trying to impress her by emulating the low-pitched Jamaican accent of scary boyfriend *Errol*?

'*NO!*' I said in a slightly higher pitch—gradually morphing my ridiculous *Errol* accent into something a little more *white* Anglo-Saxon.

Thinking quickly, I launched into the first excuse that came to mind.

'Err… well, actually Dawn… I… err, I've had a bit of a cold, YES, THAT'S IT…! I've had a *really* bad cold. In fact, the doctor said it's a miracle I could speak at all!'

'Oh, I see!' Said the ever so attractive Dawn—unconvinced, and obviously still amused.

My voice had now risen by more than an octave in a few short sentences. And still trying desperately to sound the *exact* opposite of Errol, I became the sound-a-like love-child of Michael Caine and Prince Charles—bouncing on every word from posh to Cockney, Cockney to posh. I was an accent out of control, an identity lost in a crisis, and Dawn must have thought she was talking to at least *three* different people.

'I think we're rehearsing at 4 pm,' I squealed, in a pitch that was now higher than hers.

I had completely misread Dawn's intentions. She really *did* just want to know what time the band were rehearsing that day—nothing more and nothing less. Needless to say, I felt pretty stupid afterwards.

No doubt, if Errol had ever found out I was trying

to *be* him in order to impress his girlfriend, it's extremely unlikely this book would have ever been written.

My ongoing search for identity reached bizarre new heights when I attempted a marriage proposal in the style of Police Captain *Frank Furillo,* from the classic American TV drama, *Hills Street Blues*...

It was a cold winters evening, when, armed with an uneasy swagger, and dressed in a smart suit and beige raincoat—the type worn by the aforementioned Captain—Bonnie and I entered the *Star of India* restaurant in swanky Notting Hill.

With a sparkling engagement ring stashed safely in my pocket, I imagined we were in the scene from *Hill Street Blues* where Captain Furillo sits opposite love interest—Public Defender, *Joyce Davenport* —across a softly focused candlelit table.

And then, with impeccable timing and unquestionable masculinity he asks, '*will you marry me?*'

To which *Bonnie,* in the role of Joyce Davenport replies, '*yes Frank yes...!*'

I'd reach into my jacket pocket, and without moving my eyes from hers, would slide the ring effortlessly onto the appropriate finger. No further words would be needed. The theme music and end credits would roll, and we'd step out onto a snowy

Chicago street. Again, I'd take control—just like *Frank* would—by hailing a yellow taxi cab with a single wave of the hand. Bonnie wouldn't say it out loud, but secretly I knew she'd be impressed.

But…

We were not in Chicago, or wherever Hill Street Blues was based—we were outside an Indian restaurant in Notting Hill Gate wading through filthy, ankle high snow. And as we entered *The Star of India*, it was clear that Bonnie was not in the best of moods.

'You'll love it here—*Molly* did.' I repeated casually for the umpteenth time without realising the utter, naive inappropriateness of these constant references to an ex-girlfriend.

'In fact,' I continued unwisely, 'it was Molly's favourite restaurant. They'd always give us that cosy little table over there in the corner… away from all the noise…'

*Bonnie*, now stern faced, and for some reason ready for a fight—folded her arms and looked up to acknowledge the waiter.

'Table for two please,' I announced robustly—fully expecting the waiter to reply, 'ah, Mr Slavin, we've been expecting you… Same table as usual sir?'

But instead, we were shown to the only available table in the restaurant by a disinterested waiter with language skills best described as *basic*:

'Hello—sit    down—eat—pay    bill    now —*goodbye*…'

Unfortunately, our soft-focus, candle-lit table was near the entrance—a busy thoroughfare leading to a squeaky door that when opened, put Bonnie and I squarely in the firing line of an icy blizzard reaping havoc on the pavement outside.

Even *I* could tell that Bonnie wasn't best pleased with the seating arrangements…

'I can see why *this* table was empty,' she muttered —her irritability increasing with every gust of sub-zero wind.

And to make matters worse, her chair rested on a loose floorboard that flipped her into the air whenever someone walked past.

This was not going *well*. What would Captain Frank Furillo of Hill Street Blues do in a moment of crisis like this? Probably cut to an advert for washing powder or haemorrhoid cream, or toothpaste, leaving viewers in suspense. Or perhaps he would win Joyce over with some typically smooth small talk.

Conceding that there was no obvious way of cutting to a commercial, I decided on the small talk option.

This turned out to be a mistake…

'Anyway, as I was saying, *Molly* loved it here, they'd never have given *her* this crappy table!'

Bonnie glared at me.

*The Star of India's* squeaky exit door opened, and then closed, and then opened again—finally jamming in an open position that allowed an icy blast of filthy air to leave a thin layer of frost on our Tandoori chicken. We begin to argue.

'Why did you bring me here to this dump, anyway?' Bonnie asks angrily.

'I thought you'd like it here… *Molly* did,' I replied honestly, although unwisely.

'WELL, WHY THE HELL DON'T YOU GO AND BLOODY MARRY *MOLLY* THEN?' She fires back as though I'd said something *really* bad.

This was confusing. I couldn't understand why she was so angry. After all, wasn't honesty always supposed to be the *best policy*? I began to wonder if whoever told me this, had actually been lying. Isn't life complicated enough without the extra hassle of concocting alternative variations of *truth*?

The drive home from *The Star of India* that night was tense. The silence broken only by squeaky wind-screen wiper blades struggling in vain against the hardening snow. I felt stupid and inadequate and wondered how it had all gone so wrong when I'd had such good intentions.

One day my epitaph shall read:

*Steven, much loved father, son and husband. A man for whom the road to hell was paved with good intentions.*

The autism diagnosis prompted my greatest ever unravelling of *self,* from a lifetime's overgrown tangle of twisted perception, and inauthentic belief—a search for identity bigger than any I'd previously undertaken.

It's been more than ten years since the diagnosis. And as I approach my sixth decade, I'm finally beginning to get the *hang* of the new me.

If only I could begin my life again knowing what I know now. But then, wouldn't everyone be a genius if they could relive their lives according to the wisdom of hindsight?

Perhaps I *will* call my next book, *Can I Start Again Please...*

## 35

## SUCCESS AT LAST: 1986

*A wise man once said: 'Goals that become obsessions force us to walk dangerous paths.'*

*An even wiser, wise man said: 'The line between success and failure is so fine, it can be drawn on the arse of a skinny horsefly.'*

'You're *really* on your way now,' said Bonnie, as we read through the glowing reviews of my first *solo* record.

*A WINNER! HYPNOTIC! A DANCE-FLOOR SMASH! UNFORGETTABLE!* They all said of the four-minute dance-pop record—still considered to be something of an 80s classic in its genre.

*Rhythm of Your Love* was the first record I'd written and produced alone. And with the addition of singer *Isabel Roberts* on vocals, I was convinced we'd created something the public was going to like.

For once in my life I had seen the future, and it had looked bright and exciting.

Hearing one's record blasting out of the car radio for the first time is quite simply surreal. But hearing one's record blasting out of someone *else's* car radio as they pull up alongside at the traffic lights is a sure sign that life will never be the same again.

For a few extraordinary months, my record seemed to take on a life of its own. From Glasgow to Penzance, people were buying it, and the nation's top DJ's were spinning it. Yet, all the while you wonder how long your moment in the sun will last. How high will your record climb that slippery ladder of success before, like all things, it returns to the hard reality of earth?

Driving home from the studio one night, I turned on the car radio just as the DJ with a fake American accent began his weekly chart rundown…

'Dropping to number thirty-nine are those *cool* cats of funk: *Kool and the Gang*. And rising to thirty-eight is the smooth sound of *Overjoyed* by *Stevie Wonder…*'

And as I made my way through the dark city night, my disappointment rose with the announcement of each ascending chart position that was not occupied by *my* record.

Time and numbers were running out, and hope

was fading fast as the DJ revealed those lucky artists who'd made it into the top twenty—and still, no mention of my record. Surely now, the game was up, and my brief moment of minor glory at the bottom of the chart was as good as it was ever going to get.

The DJ continued to notify his late night audience of a descending *Michael Jackson,* a rising *Whitney Houston* and an unchanged *George Benson*—who'd been stuck at number *twenty-two* for the second poptastic week in a row.

*Well,* I thought, with an unattractive hint of bitterness, *at least good ole George was stuck at a respectable chart position.*

The only place *I* was stuck at, was a set of red traffic lights that seemed determined never to turn green again. But they did, and just as the DJ—now in a state of embarrassing transatlantic frenzy, was ready to announce the *Top-Ten.*

'…And in at number two, with a bullet, is this week's fastest climber, *Rhythm of Your Love*!'

I did not scream, and I did not swear. Instead, I calmly pulled over to the side of the road for a while to reflect on my strange new reality.

Did the DJ with the fake American accent *really* just say we were at number *two* in the chart? And above *less* popular records by Stevie Wonder, Janet

Jackson, Michael Jackson, Kool and the Gang, George Benson and Whitney Houston...?

Apparently, he did.

## My Strange Reaction to Good News

When my thoughts get too big and exciting, and I cannot control them, I flap my hands when no one is watching, and pace the floor like a tiger that hasn't eaten for days.

*Bad* news, on the other hand, makes me feel tired and lethargic. All I can do is sleep—to switch off, to reboot my brain.

*Happy*, was not the emotion I felt when *Rhythm of your Love* was at the peak of its popularity.

'Relax, enjoy your moment in the sun,' people would say. But I couldn't. I knew success of this kind was fleeting, and may never come again.

I was reminded of the short-lived magic of a childhood Christmas morning. Soon it would all be over. The decorations would come down and the dullness of *real* life would return for a further twelve months.

Gradually, I watched my record's inevitable descent from two, to thirty-two—passing, on the way down—a rising *Chaka Khan,* and a still hovering *George Benson,* before disappearing off the chart altogether and into the nations cut-price bargain bins.

Still, I made some money from that record, *and*

learnt some useful things about life, people, and the business of music.

- Lesson number one: Never assume that people will do what you think they should.
- Lesson number two: Never forget lesson number one…

In 1987 I became aware of the growing trend towards computerised recording studio technology. This presented a way of working that could have been designed specifically for autistic musicians like me.

This new technology allowed me to record all the instruments alone. I invested my earnings in equipment and turned my little childhood bedroom into a small recording studio. Here I would write the songs and record my demo's. These would later be finished off at either *Herne Place*, or *Jacobs*—both top-flight studios in the heart of the Surrey countryside.

Assisting me in my obsessive quest for musical perfection was the legendary recording engineer *Ken Thomas*.

Back then, I would enter a recording studio with the reverence afforded to a place of worship. I lived for the prospect of crafting supreme sonic magic in that high-tech nirvana—note by note, and sound by sound. I'd become so lost in the detail and control made possible by this new technology, that the budget conscious record company boss would often remind me that…

*Micro-managing every atom of sound was costing him a fortune in studio time. And the public would neither notice, or care, if that G Minor chord lasted 2.5 milliseconds longer than it did on the previous verse!*

'Look, Steve,' he'd say. 'I'm sure it *won't* affect sales… just get the damn song finished, and let's get out of here!'

By 5 am, the record company boss who had been so full of enthusiasm the previous morning, was slumped and dishevelled on the sofa at the back of the studio. Meanwhile, the affable Ken Thomas, of *Queen, Bowie* and *The Damned* fame—was drifting in and out of sleep in his swivel-chair behind the mixing desk.

For eighteen-hours straight, Ken had pushed faders, twisted knobs and flicked switches to facilitate my obsessional quest for perfection.

'OK,' I said, reluctantly.

'I'll just do *one* more take on that guitar part, and we'll call it a *day!*'

Seventeen takes later, we called it a *day.* I walked out into the early morning sunshine wishing I could've had just one more go at recording that final note on the chorus. Everyone agreed on how great the track sounded. But all I could think about was that final note.

Many years later when I broke the news of my autism diagnosis to music industry colleagues, no one was particularly surprised.

The general consensus was…

'We always thought you were strangely intense and obsessive about your music—now we know why…'

## 36

### SEPTEMBER 1987

By any standards, September 1987 was a *very* good month.

It was the month I signed my biggest ever recording contract, wrote a song for 80s pop sensation *Sinitta*, and to top it all, married the love of my life, *Bonnie*.

And as the plane sped along the runway destined for Crete—our honeymoon destination—it felt as though *this* time, we truly *were* on our way.

After five months of frustrating negotiations with Harley Music Limited (not to be confused with other companies of the same name!) my solicitor called me with the good news…

'I think we've pushed them as far as we can, let's go ahead and sign the deal.'

With the benefit of hindsight, I would have been better off taking a few thousand pounds, flushing it down the toilet, and have the record company boss scribble a few lines on a paper napkin instead. But anyhow, the ink at the bottom of the fifty-two-page agreement was dry, and it was time to start making some hit records.

The thing that really excited me about Harley Music, were their international connections. Especially in America, where they had good ties with the teams around *Madonna,* and *Debbie Gibson.* Remember her?

A quick scan around Harley's office walls revealed every type of music industry award imaginable. How could I *not* be impressed and flattered when, on the strength of my minor hit with *Rhythm of Your Love* the previous year, Harley approached me, and offered an all encompassing five-year contract? They were now my Management, my Publisher, *and* my Record Company.

'Sign with us, and you'll make millions,' they said.

'Just write them, and we'll sell them…'

So, I did. I just wrote, and wrote, and wrote—all day, every day, and all night, every night—in their well equipped recording studio, until I had more songs than I could count.

My job, as Harley music's *in-house,* writer, producer, was to come up with hit songs for the artists signed to the company—many of whom had already achieved respectable chart success.

To this end, my first record was a mid-tempo, pop-soul affair, by the name of *Sweet, Like Honey to a Bee*. And the artist lined up to sing it was the gloriously named *Pearly Gates*—an African-American lady from Alabama who's previous record *Action* had made her a favourite on the UK club scene. My song, *Sweet, Like Honey to a Bee* was designed to broaden her appeal, and to push her career to even greater heights.

On release, an enormous box arrived at the record company office. Inside were dozens of honey-filled jars with labels stating...

*Sweet, Like Honey to a Bee—The new single from Pearly Gates.*

The promotional jars of honey were sent out to all the radio stations along with copies of the record, in the hope of creating a *buzz* in the industry. And the strategy almost worked. *Sweet* climbed into the bottom half of the national chart, stayed there for a while, and then disappeared. But at least it was another record in the chart for me, and I did make some reasonable money from all of the radio play on the BBC.

My next record for Harley Music suffered a fate that had me jumping for joy, and fighting back the tears almost simultaneously. For reasons that will become apparent, it's probably best that I don't name the artist involved.

'Great news *Steve*!' Exclaimed Harley's infectiously upbeat boss. 'The records come in at number 26…!'

My heart pounded, as I paced frantically from one end of his office to the other, barely able to contain my excitement. I must call Bonnie to tell her the good news, she'll be thrilled, I thought, reaching for the office phone…

But then, suddenly the office door flew open, and in marched a steaming *Richie White*—second in charge, and hard-nut veteran of the 1960s music scene. An era when contract negotiations occasionally involved dangling uncooperative managers from second-floor windows.

'The bloody record… ! It's just been pulled off the bloody chart by bloody *Gallup,'* he screamed —thumping the desk with his powerful fist. (*Gallop* were the organisation responsible for regulating the UK music chart at the time).

Richie continued in biting Michael Caine tones…

'Ronnie, from the bloody sales team, was caught buying up all the copies in bloody Scotland. And now I've had Gallup on the bloody phone accusing us of bloody cheating. I told that bloody stupid Ronnie… *be discreet when you're buying up the bloody records Ronnie.* But *no*, not Ronnie…! Not bloody Ronnie! *He* walks into bloody *Woolworths* with bags full of the same record from every bloody record store in bloody Glasgow… *and* shows them to the bloody manager*!'*

This tactic of record companies buying up their own records from stores to artificially inflate sales was common practice back then. But this time the strategy had backfired, and Richie was obviously *bloody* angry.

I, on the other hand, was bloody devastated. Should I even tell Bonnie that we were in the top-thirty for all of five minutes? And now, because of bloody *Ronnie*, Gallup had demoted the bloody record from *26* to *135*?

\* \* \*

For months I barely saw Bonnie, and when I did, I was so tired and stressed out from the non-stop recording, that I may as well have not been there.

Once, after a continuous twenty-four-hour studio session I was driven—along with artists, *Keren and Chelle Poole*—to the ITV building in Camden for a 7 am promotional appearance on breakfast TV with presenter *Ann Diamond*—remember her?

Then, exhausted to the point of hallucination, we returned to the studio for a further eighteen-hours of recording.

'Don't worry,' I kept reassuring Bonnie. 'One day we'll have a big house in the country. The sacrifice will be worth it in the end, you'll see…'

The following April 1988, my all expenses paid trip to New York to record a new single with American singer *Lee Prentiss* was interrupted by the arrival of a gorgeous little coffee-skinned child called *Sophie.*

Next to Bonnie's hospital bed was a large bouquet of flowers, and a card from the staff at Harley Music. Everyone had written goodwill messages inside. Even bloody *Ronnie* had—in his own way—managed to scrawl something memorable:

*'If it moves, funk it…!* Love Ronnie.'

Someone else wrote: 'To Bonnie and Steve—congrats on your greatest ever production.'

And as the sun went down on that rare April day, I carried our delicate little bundle of warm joy to the window of the maternity ward. I held her up to view the jagged London skyline for the first time, and whispered…

*'Welcome to the world my little one—welcome to the world.'*

## 37

# CILLA AND THE FRISBEE

Within weeks of Sophie's birth, the record company flew me, and the band out to Spain to appear on—of all things—*The Cilla Black Show*.

Also along for the trip were some label *execs* and a film crew to shoot the music video for the new single.

Notable band members on this gig, included, drummer *Frank Tontoh* of George Michael and Amy Winehouse fame. And on keyboards, the now BAFTA-winning composer *Simon Hal*e.

We'd perform at night, and during the blistering *Costa Del Sol* days, Simon and I would play frisbee by the pool and drink bottles of San Miguel. We'd talk for hours about music, relationships and all the wonderful things we hoped to achieve one day. I haven't seen Simon for many years, but by all accounts, he has truly surpassed his poolside dreams.

Some evenings before a show, I'd call Bonnie from the hotel lobby to tell her how things were going...

'It feels like big things are going to happen for us soon—*really* soon. It's all so exciting!'

I'd say goodnight to a hopeful Bonnie, and a gurgling, month-old Sophie, and make my way to the backstage area of the arena.

'We're *on* soon Steve,' someone shouts.

My stomach begins to churn, knowing that shortly, I will, again, become a forgetful stage-strutting warrior high above the facing crowd—and what was that first chord again?

Our short set is over in a flash, and all too soon we're bowing, and shouting *GOODNIGHT SPAIN* to the packed amphitheatre.

'*MORE, MORE,*' they shout. But we *have* no more, and leave Cilla to work her Scouse charm on the full-house of tomato-skinned English tourists…

Back in London after the Spanish trip, my recording schedule continued at a relentless pace.

I lived, breathed, ate and drank music. My brain had become little more than a generator of rhyming lyrics and melodic ideas. Every cell of grey matter was engaged in the pursuit of musical excellence and the winning lottery ticket of a hit record.

But, so utterly intoxicated was I by the drive for success, that I was seeing even *less* of Bonnie than ever. And although the average neurotypical may have noticed the strain this was having on their relationship—I did not, and ploughed on regardless.

Surely, one day the hard work would pay off, and the story would have a happy ending. *Surely*, one day, Bonnie and I would look back and think—*times were tough back then, but the sacrifice was worth it, just look at us now…*

## Atlantic Records

The highlight, or lowlight—depending on how you see it—of my time with Harley Music, was the album I co-wrote and co-produced for singing sisters *Karen and Chelle Poole.*

They were the daughters of *Tremeloes* heartthrob *Brian Poole*—a very big star in the 1960s.

With the first few tracks completed, a deal was struck with Atlantic Records in New York. This was for two singles followed by an album, if sales were good.

Having my name appear on that famous orange and green label was a huge thrill. Now I could boast that I was record company mates with Genesis, Led Zeppelin, and The Rolling Stones. But in reality, my rock heroes existed in worlds so distant from mine, that being with the same record company meant very little. It wasn't like I could hang out with Mick and the boys, or jam with Jimmy Page whenever I felt like it.

Our first single for Atlantic was a poppy little number entitled *Sugar Daddy*—a song we'd originally recorded with 80s singer *Sinitta*—her, of *So Macho* and X Factor fame.

Unfortunately, *Sugar Daddy* was released to a decidedly unimpressed American public, and sales were poor. Although, for a while, I held on to the faintest flicker of hope that *Sugar Daddy's* apparent popularity in the gay bars of Houston, Texas may spread into the heterosexual mainstream. But, of course, it didn't.

Still, at least the record did quite well in the UK, France and Japan. And when it was discovered that Keren and Chelle had a famous father, the brief media storm led to a number of prime-time TV spots that helped push the record even further up the UK chart.

Yet, for all the hype and the dream deals with Atlantic and Sony, sales were slower than expected. And to make matters worse, financial cracks were beginning to appear in Harley Music's creaking infrastructure.

The talk around the office was no longer about chart positions and radio play. It was about unpaid wages, and redundancy.

'Steve, come in, take a seat,' said the unusually sombre, record company boss.

'It's about that money we owe you from the Sony contract in Japan, well, you *can't* have it… *ever*. We're no longer in business.'

Then—in a flashback to the *dangle 'em out of a window* style of negotiation—second-in-charge Richie White announces, 'yeah, and we're not letting you out of your contract either!'

This was not good news. Richie was informing me that I was little more than a company asset in a bankruptcy case, and therefore property of the Official Receiver.

Harley owed me *thousands*. In fact, enough for a small deposit on the house I promised Bonnie we'd own one day. In addition, I was tied to a worthless contract that rendered me unable to work in the industry for a further three years. How was I ever going to break this news to Bonnie? She had believed in me unconditionally, and I'd let her down.

I couldn't face going straight home after the meeting. Instead, I sat on a park bench opposite a couple of old drunks. They were hurling friendly abuse at each other whilst guzzling strong cider from large plastic bottles.

Life, it seems, was not going so well for them either. But at least they seemed happy in their inebriation.

How had everything gone so horribly wrong? And more importantly, what would I do next? I was almost thirty years of age, burnt out, penniless, and depressed. I would not have the emotional strength to start again.

If the dream really was over, then what would I do? Music was all I knew.

Should I retrain as a social worker? Or get a job in a bank? I'm useless at remembering things, and get really confused when counting money, so neither of those jobs would be any good. I could become a London Taxi driver like dad. He makes a reasonable living. But then I can't drive to the end of my road without getting lost, so that wouldn't work either. How about becoming a shelf-stacker in a supermarket? Granted, I would find it a challenge to recall where to stack the beans and toilet paper, but with some practise I could probably hack it. But this wasn't the life I'd promised Bonnie. She deserved so much more than to be the wife of a lowly paid shelf-stacker...

It was getting dark, and the park warden looked as though he was about to lock up for the night. So, drained of all emotion, I left the two old drunks to their unintelligible sentences, and continued my journey home to Bonnie.


## Three Months Later: A Painful Irony

Still locked into a contract that meant I couldn't record for any other company, I was forced to take my first non-music related job since leaving *Goldbergs Fabrics* in 1980.

My job was to visit convenience stores in the London area, and replace the old price stickers on the side of ice-cream freezers with updated versions. This was a job I hated, but it was better than nothing, and it didn't involve too much thinking.

Then, one day, I was kneeling on a dirty shop floor in rundown Hackney—scraping filthy black glue from the side of an old white freezer.

Suddenly, from the radio by the cash till, I heard the transatlantic tones of super-hyped Capital Radio DJ *Pat Sharp*…

'Next up, it's *Sugar Daddy*… the smash hit from *Keren and Chelle Poole*…'

Not only was the *king* of Capital Radio, Pat Sharp, playing *my* record, it had apparently become so popular amongst young Londoners that he'd made it the subject of a competition.

Giggling teenage girls would phone in to the

show, and sing their own version of the lyrics whilst the song was playing. The best version would receive a prize of some description.

And as the happy little slice of Euro pop-trash blasted out into the grubby East London convenience store, I could feel within me, every possible emotion experienced by *any* human, since we first emerged as single-celled amoebas from that murky primordial swamp.

Should I be happy to hear my song on day time radio? Or, devastated knowing that even if it sold a million copies I would not receive a penny, ever?

I honestly didn't know whether to laugh or cry.

I finished pressing home the new ice-cream poster just as *Sugar Daddy* faded into *Madonna, or Tina Turner, or George Michael*—I can't remember now.

Then from behind me I heard…

'It's not on straight, mate, you'll have to take it off and do it again.'

It was the voice of the Asian shopkeeper who seemed to think he was inspecting a wall of fine art in the National Gallery!

I felt like shouting back at him '*who the f\*\*k do you think you're talking to…? Don't you know that was my song on the radio just now…?!*'

I shrugged my shoulders and stormed out of the shop without saying a word—with an angry convenience store owner shouting after me in loud *Gujarati*.

This was the *pits*, and I was up to my greying hair line in it's depressing mire.

I sat in the car across the street from the store for a while, wondering how it had all come to this.

Perhaps music wasn't the right job for me after all. Just because your *good* at something, doesn't necessarily mean you should try and turn it into a career. But what else could I do? Spend the rest of my life replacing ice-cream posters on dirty old freezers?

No, I wasn't done yet. I had to find the strength somehow to start again. To keep the promise I'd once made to Bonnie, and to repay her trust in me. I still wanted that lovely big house in the country with a lake, and ducks, and rolling terraces, and a white piano—just like the one John Lennon played when he sang *Imagine* to Yoko…

I would make it big one day—or, I would die trying. This, would be my *only* plan.

A few years later, Keren and Chelle re-emerged as the highly successful *Alisha's Attic*—aided by the fine production skills of the Eurythmics' Dave Stewart.

I met him once, briefly, at an industry gathering in 2006.

'Nice work on those girls *Dave*,' I thought of saying, but didn't bother in the end. What would be the point? By then he was working with Ringo Starr,

Mick Jagger and Stevie Nicks. He certainly didn't need any morale-boosting praise from *me*…

## 38

## AFTER THE APOCALYPSE: 1990

Someone Once Said:

*'Gullibility is no excuse for stupidity.'*
Unfortunately, I always seem to be on the wrong
end of this inconvenient equation.

If I were to describe the 1980s as my *nearly*-years, I
would call the proceeding ten, my *utterly-lost-years*.
A period defined by destroyed confidence and poor
decision making. A stifling concoction of inner
conflict from which nothing good could ever grow.

My *utterly-lost-years* would propel me off course,
and spinning into ever more hopeless career orbits
with every desperate and ill-conceived decision.

Firstly, I shall refer you to ex-pop mogul, and ever
present TV personality of my youth, *Jonathan King*.

Jonathan had sold a staggering forty-million

records, discovered *Genesis,* and was, for many years, one of the music industry's leading opinion-makers.

I remember well, the evening he called me from New York…

'Hi Steve… it's me, *Jonathan*, I'm in New York. It's about that *faaabulous* song of yours *Faded to Grey.* I want it to represent Great Britain in the Euro-vision Song Contest next year. Let's hook up when I'm back in London after Christmas… okay —*faaabulous*!'

I turned to Bonnie and said, 'you'll never guess who that was? It was Jonathan King, he wants *Faded to Grey* to represent Great Britain in the Eurovision Song Contest…!'

Bonnie did not reply.

After all we'd been through—the high hopes, false dawns and broken promises, her reaction to any flicker of hope had understandably become little more than a disbelieving raised eyebrow.

We struggled through yet another penniless Christmas season, and I prayed the *fabulous* one's return in the new year would bring a much needed change of fortune.

At the time, Jonathan was head honcho at Great Britain's Eurovision Song Committee, and could *help* a song progress through the various stages of voting and on to the live finals.

Things were progressing nicely, and true to his word, Jonathan had pushed *Faded to Grey* through the thousands of submissions, and into the final sixteen. Next, Jonathan would use his *fabulously* weighty influence to push the song through to the live finals—what could possibly go wrong…?

## The BBC News

I'm cleaning up in the kitchen, when, from the TV set I hear…

> *Pop producer Jonathan King was arrested today on a number of charges. Mr King denies the allegations, and vows to clear his name…*

For a few seconds, the newsreader's words failed to register, and I continued to scrape away at the burnt remnants of the previous day's roasting tray. But, then, slowly, the implications of this badly timed slice of breaking news began to dawn.

I turned towards the TV set to see images of Jonathan pushing his way through a crowd of eager press, hungry for a quote.

My initial reaction was:

*I wonder if he'll still be able to get my song through to the live finals of Eurovision from prison?*

Needless to say, Eurovision came and went, as would Jonathan's fabulous liberty sometime later…

\* \* \*

Somewhere around 1996, I became involved in the making of a spoof rap-record. This desperate piece of trash was based on the interview Princess Diana gave to Martin Bashir. In the interview she'd said, '*there are three of us in this marriage... I am a free-spirit.*'

The record company hired a Diana sound-a-like to replicate her voice, and a Diana look-a-like to play her in the music video.

And whilst the controversial record didn't exactly take the music charts by storm, it *did* succeed in creating a huge wave of publicity—both in the press, and on TV.

At one stage, TV crews from around the world were queuing up to conduct interviews with the song's producers. They all wanted to know, 'did Diana *really* appear on the record? And if she did, what was the response from the Queen and Prince Charles?'

Perhaps the comedic lowlight of this particular stage of my floundering career, was when mum called me to ask:

'*STEVEN,* WHAT HAVE YOU DONE THIS TIME?'

'Err, what do you mean mum?' I replied.

'Well, the newspaper says the *Queen* is suing the producers of the *Diana* record...!'

I assured my mother that no one involved in the record was likely to be hung for treason. And that it was probably just a story planted by hotshot PR guru

Max Clifford—the man hired to create a media frenzy around the record.

A year later, Lady Di was dead—killed in a Parisian tunnel. I felt sleazy and ashamed at my involvement in a record that only added to the incessant press intrusion into her life. An intrusion that may ultimately have contributed to her death.

* * *

Continuing on with my tales of gullibility and desperation, I will describe briefly, another bruising encounter with one of life's unscrupulous chancers. I shall refer to the perpetrator as *Terence Brown*.

Somewhere around 1992, I was lured into a recording studio business with the smooth talking Mr Brown.

According to him, he had all the top people in the music business on speed dial. And with the flick of a button could summon up Michael Jackson, or Whitney Houston, or Quincy Jones.

In some ways, this was not so unbelievable. I did, in fact know people that had worked with Michael Jackson, Whitney Houston and Quincy Jones. And anyhow, I was desperate for a break, and decided to take a chance with the convincing Mr Brown.

Together we rented a studio space in North London and started to turn out some pretty good music. For a while, the first, tentative, green shoots of a career revival began to break through the surface of my barren wasteland.

But then—and with me there is always a —*but then…*

## The Studio Phone Rings…

'Hello, this is Detective Hazel from the Fraud Squad. I'm calling about your business partner *Terence Brown*. He's been arrested and charged with multiple counts of embezzlement.'

Apparently, Terence had been funding our studio, by emptying the bank accounts of unfortunate women all over Europe.

'*You* are not a suspect,' continued Detective Hazel. 'But we may need to question you as a witness.'

The story made a big, sensational splash on the front pages of the nation's tabloids. And once again, mum was on the phone asking, 'isn't that the man you work with *Steven?*'

'Yes, mum, it is, but don't worry. Terence's international trail of women—left broken and embezzled—was nothing to do with me.'

And, as for his, *amazing music biz contacts?* Well, of course he had none. It was all lies.

On hearing this bizarre news, Bonnie reminded me that she, '*never did trust that guy anyway*.' And that, '*Genuinely* successful people never smell of sweat, and that Terence absolutely *stunk*!'

Of course, Bonnie was right—*again*. But such are my character judging skills, that if someone tells me they're best friends with Michael Jackson—who am I to disbelieve them?

Needless to say, my fraudulent ex-studio partner went to jail, and I moved on to other disastrous business relationships.

There was a rather incredible addendum to this story.

Sometime later, Hollywood film director Michael Winner—in his *True Crime Stories* TV series—featured a dramatisation of Terence's criminal activity. Many of the reconstructed events were based on the time we were recording studio partners. And as the credits rolled at the end of the program, I shook my head in self-castigating disbelief and repeated quietly to myself—*brilliant Steve… just brilliant.* How could I be so damn naive?

I'd wasted two years, and wished I'd listened to Bonnie when she'd angrily stated…

'Why do you keep working with all of these useless idiots? All they do is use you—when are you going to wake up…?'

She was right. But I wasn't ready to listen.

It would, in fact, be many years before I'd begin

to *wake up*. And in the meantime, there were still a surprising number of wrong paths and cul-de-sacs to explore before the autistic penny dropped in 2008.

Still, the 1990s were not *all* bad.

The decade began with the arrival of a beautiful, blue-eyed baby girl called *Beth*.

Her hair was brown, bronze and golden, and would soon grow into wild, unbrushable corkscrews that had people staring in awe.

Bonnie and I were frequently stopped in the street by strangers, who'd gaze admiringly at the diverse contents of our double baby-stroller. The wide genetic soup cooked up by Bonnie's African and Anglo-Saxon heritage, spiced with my Ashkenazi, Jewish roots, resulted in daughters that, at various stages of development, looked completely unrelated.

I'd often joke that we'd considered having another child just to see what it would look like…

Perhaps a Barbra Streisand look-a-like with a Beyonce posteria and a thick afro. Or a dead ringer for Will Smith, but with pale skin, blue eyes and a Mel Brooks voice… Who knows? With *our* gene pool anything's possible.

Other highlights from the decade I'd rather forget, were the albums I recorded with Adrian Lee of *Genesis* spin-off group *Mike and the Mechanics*. And also the singles I made with Kylie Minogue's Grammy award winning producer *Philip Larsen*. But all the while my ever present mid-level depression would take my energy and dampen my spirit. I'd survive on willpower, caffeine and prozac, whilst feeling wholly inadequate in the company of such high achievers.

But then I began to realise that god-given talent was not the *only* reason people become successful in the music business—or, in fact, in any sphere of life.

I used to think that fame and fortune rested solely on the backs of my songs. All I had to do was keep writing them, and everything else would fall into place. This long-standing assumption turned out to be naive and incorrect. In reality, the mechanics of success rely more heavily on the very things most people with autism find challenging.

For example—decision making, and choosing the *right* people to work with. Knowing who to trust, and being able to fathom another's intent.

My successful colleagues were also blessed with a distinct lack of social fear.

Whilst I'd shrink hopelessly into my pathetic shell at the mere suggestion of a prime networking opportunity, my high achieving friends would positively jump at the chance to mingle with the great and the good of the music industry. My successful *friends* appeared to have been born with the gift of looking completely comfortable in their skins. They did not fidget like a seven-year-old-child who needs to pee, and did not rock from side to side when they felt uncomfortable during a conversation with someone important. They did not say sorry every thirty-seconds, and were *really* good at making eye contact —skills I struggle with to this day.

The music business is little more than a network of people who know other people. Relationships are forged in wine bars and social gatherings—environments likely to cause anxiety in the average autistic.

Dad once told me, 'it's not *what* you know, it's *who* you know.'

I remember being quick to dismiss this as meaningless cliché. But he was absolutely correct. Success doesn't happen in a vacuum. You simply *have* to get out and meet people if you want to get anywhere in life.

If I'd known about autism in 1990, perhaps I would have spent more time working on my social skills, and less time obsessing over the lyrics to some new song the world didn't need.

But then as I've probably mentioned elsewhere in this book—with the benefit of hindsight everyone can be a genius.

## 39

# OCD AND THE MILLENNIUM BUG

'SIX… FIVE… FOUR… THREE… TWO… ONE… *HAPPY NEW YEAR!'* screamed the elated throng of ecstatic party goers. Suddenly the sky above North London exploded into multi-coloured showers of short-lived glitter. Everywhere, rockets fired and fizzed above our heads—filling the cold January air with the smell of burnt phosphor.

This was the sound of *normal* people enjoying themselves. Was I really the *only* person at the party genetically incapable of having fun? Perhaps there were others that, given the choice, would have also secretly preferred a quiet night at home with some hot cocoa—reflecting on the twelve-months that had just become *last year?*

Instead, drunk and sweaty acquaintances were soaking my face with hot and sloppy kisses.

'Happy new-year *Steven*!'

'Yes, and a happy New Year to you too,' I'd reply with my best fake smile—trying to avoid any further bodily contact.

Parties are my OCD hell. All that hugging, and handshaking, and endless bathroom visits to scrub my contaminated skin from the sweat and saliva of joyous revellers.

In a perfect OCD world, I would only shake another's hand, if, I could be absolutely sure, the person to whom it belongs, conforms to the highest standards of moral, and personal hygiene. And from an autistic point of view, I would encourage people not to speak so loudly. This only encourages everyone else to talk even louder so they can be heard over whoever lost control of their volume in the first place. And whilst we're discussing *volume,* some prior warning of an upcoming spike in the auditory landscape wouldn't go amiss either. This would give me time to block my ears before my entire nervous system explodes —*again*.

I stand awkwardly in the corner with my sand-wich and orange juice watching Bonnie. She's where she *always* is—right in the centre of things. By default, the life and soul of every party.

She's like a beautiful magnet—surrounded, and dancing, and singing along to *Celebration* by Kool and the Gang. Bonnie's always been a good mover, I was never a match for her on the dance floor, but at least I know the correct words to all of those party songs she likes to sing at the top of her voice.

Still, she seems to be having fun, and that makes me happy.

And whilst we're on the topic of *fun*. I should mention that this is something Bonnie says I need to have *more* of. But then, I have tried having *fun* in the past, and I didn't enjoy it. It felt fake and empty. And because *fun* invariably happens in the company of other people, by its very definition, having fun could never actually be... well... *fun*.

And, in any case, how exactly does *fun* compare to those other much sought after human conditions —*contentment* and *happiness?* There appears to be so many things to consider before entertaining the idea of pursuing the state of *fun*. But now, I'm probably doing the thing Bonnie says I need to do a lot *less* of —over thinking things... again.

Personally, I've always viewed New Year celebratory events as rather sad affairs. I'm confused by the outpouring of apparent joy that never fails to wither in the cold light of a hung-over morning. Do these purveyors of temporary jubilation not realise that on January 1st their lives will be exactly the same as they were the previous day?

But there I go again—over-thinking things until I give myself a headache.

My *next* New Year's resolution will be to take Bonnie's advice a bit more seriously, and not get so intense about everything—to smile a bit more, and to *go with the flow.* Whatever *that* means...

* * *

It's 2 am, and the party is in full swing.

But wait a minute... I suddenly thought. Wasn't the *Millennium Bug* supposed to have started reaping digital chaos across the civilised world by now? I was relying on this particular doomsday scenario to save me from another year's drudgery and depression?

Were we not led to believe that computers would be incapable of processing the date *01-01-2000?* And that aeroplanes would fall from the sky? Nuclear missiles would launch automatically, and life as we'd known it would come to an end?

At 3 am, I stepped out onto an apocalypse-free North London street. And taking a mighty gasp of resigned air, I looked up into the icy-black sky, and remembered that, for the most part, *change* happens at the speed of drying paint. We fight our way through life's muddy trenches one day at a time, gaining an inch here, or losing a centimetre *there*—knowing that we can only ever hope to chart our progress through the lens of time's retrospective wisdom.

Suddenly, there's a huge bang and the sky explodes! Could this be it...? But no, the sky falls dark again, and I realise that it was just some fool letting off a random firework for a laugh...

By 4 am, I realised that we were probably heading towards another unexciting false dawn. Either those highly paid software engineers had done a really good job of saving the world, or the conspiracy theorists had sold me a cruel, fake dream.

I looked around the emptying room, where no more than a handful of dedicated middle-aged party lovers continued to dance as though it were still 1999. Or, by the looks of things—*1978*. These happy groovers were not thinking about a post-apocalyptic world, or the threat of accidental nuclear holocaust. They were simply living for the moment—something I wished I could do occasionally.

Bonnie says that if I pretend hard enough to be *happy,* then I will actually become *happy*. Or to quote her more directly: 'Act as if, feel as if, be as if.'

But I am useless at producing fake happiness. My fake-smile-face is reminiscent of a constipated newborn wincing in pain. Pretending to be happy makes me feel like a sad liar—empty and fraudulent. I'll take the alternative solitary state of quiet contentment *any* day of the week.

\* \* \*

On January 1st I got out of bed and scoured the news channels.

Bleary eyed, I clung to the last vestiges of hope that somewhere in the world, digital meltdown had occurred, and was about to spread to London and change my life forever.

But no, just endlessly repeating footage on Sky News of happy, drunk people kissing strangers and dancing in cold fountains.

Happy New Year, you cold wet fools—Happy New Year…

## 40

## THE IMPOSSIBLE ART OF CONVERSATION

*Age 7:*

*I was trying to speak to mum, but my words lost their meaning and became gibberish around my tangled tongue.*

It's easy to spot a fellow autistic in full conversational flow:

- Body language—a*wkward.*
- Eyes—*focused anywhere, but on yours.*
- Speech—*jagged and rambling.*

Conversation exhausts me. There is so much to think about. Am I speaking too loudly? Too quietly? Too much? Not enough? Is the other person bored? Angry? Interested? Should I force myself to make eye contact with the person I'm speaking with? And once eye-contact has been established, should I occasionally unfix my gaze and look at the ceiling? Or the floor? Or is it better to keep it simple and fix your eyes on theirs with a laser-like focus until the conversation ends? Or is that called *staring,* and considered intense and creepy?

For me, the ideal conversation is a one-way-street on which I am the sole driver of an unstoppable car hurtling earnestly towards a vague conclusion.

I think it, and I say it. I am a switch jammed either on or off. A tap that is either fully open, or fully closed. A flow of verbal consciousness that starts and never ends…

'All you've done is *talk* since we left home. When can I have a turn to speak?' Bonnie protests from the front passenger seat of the car.

Apparently, for ten, rush hour miles she has not been able to get a word in, and (quite understandably) is *not* very happy about this.

In fact, I'd become so wrapped up in getting my point across, I'd forgotten she was even in the car. But I don't admit this.

I try to explain that if my *speech train* stops mid-transit, it will have to go all the way back to the station, and begin the journey again. But even my explanation of *why* I take so long to say anything, prevents her from speaking for a further twenty minutes.

I'm not sure whether Bonnie recognises the irony of this. I'm not sure I always do either.

\* \* \*

It's just that I could never get past the inherent weirdness of standing face to face with another human— firing words at each other for some unpredetermined length of time, whilst staring at each other's eyes, or foreheads, or noses, or wherever *normal* people stare when they're engaged in conversation.

Generally, my attention is taken more by the mechanics of an interaction than it is by efficiently decoding its content.

Words arrive at my ears in vague, disjointed waves. They disappear on entry, like sand draining through grasping fingers. And the few fleeting words that *do* make it through to my short term memory, are then reverse engineered into an approximation of the speakers probable intent. But this is a lengthy process, and I often find myself replying to a comment made three sentences earlier.

Quickly, my thoughts become muddled, and my mental energy depleted. I escape the interaction and find a quiet space where I can switch off for a few minutes to regain some clarity.

For me, the only thing trickier than understanding a conversation, is ending one.

Is it best to finish with a hilarious sound bite? Or

perhaps a few words of unchallengeable wisdom? Whichever approach I decide to take, it's vitally important that once I've delivered my *best line,* I walk away immediately, in case I decide to go *off-script* and make some idiotic comment that undoes all the good work.

The downside of this approach to ending a conversation, is that each final sound bite must be delivered with the theatrical skill of an Oscar winning actor, a great philosopher, or an award winning comedic genius. I am none of these things. Just a guy with social and communication difficulties trying not to look stupid.

Once, as a teenager, I remember vowing never to speak to anyone *ever* again. I later revised this to, *only* speaking when I had something really good to say, thus lessening the chance of straying off-topic, or saying something I'd later regret.

For people with autism, conversation can be a slippery tightrope walk on a *very* windy day, high above an unforgiving neurotypical planet. The risk of falling from the wobbly wire of *social acceptability* takes extraordinary effort and concentration. And the fear of *not getting it right,* makes the risk of inter-acting with others, a far less favourable option than spending time alone, engaged in activities we have some control over.

Paradoxically, whilst my writing often contains carefully crafted sentences laced with generous lashings of flowery metaphor, I am always likely to be nonplussed by the ambiguity of others.

This is especially true when someone enquires into the state of my health…

*'Great to see you Steve! How have you been?'*

This is a question I find confusing. How much detail am I being asked to provide? And to which period of time are they referring?

Should I mention the headache I had last Friday? Or the hay fever that incapacitated me the previous July?

I would prefer the question to be…

*Hi Steve, great to see you! How were you today between the hours of 9:30 am and 10:30 am?*

Now *that* is a question to which I could give a really accurate answer…

Also, my overuse of the word, 'sorry,' is another way of unintentionally driving people to a very dark place. It's my favourite *get out of jail* word, and I use it frequently to cover myself *just in case* I've unwittingly said something offensive during a conversation…

'*Sorry* if I'm rambling on too much. *Sorry* if I'm keeping you from something more important than talking to *me*, *Sorry* for my overuse of the word *sorry.*

*Sorry* in case I say something inappropriate during this, or any other discourse—past, present or future.'

And then comes my post-conversation self-analysis. This will be at least as tortuous as the discussion I'm analysing…

*I bet they thought I was stupid, boring, childish and needy. I bet they'd wished I hadn't rambled on for ages about my new camera lens, when they clearly had zero interest in photography, other than sharing the odd selfie on Facebook.*

And so continues the endlessly nagging loop of self-criticism until my next bruising interaction.

Yet, despite all of this, there *are* those who claim to enjoy my slightly unusual musings on the world.

I remind them—at least a dozen times during the encounter—that although my conversational style may be fun in short bursts, I would, without doubt, drive them, absolutely, completely insane, if they had to spend any length of time in my company. An observation Bonnie would have little trouble testifying to in court, if dysfunctional communication skills ever became a criminal offence.

In 2016, and after weeks of auditory testing at London's *Ear Nose and Throat Hospital,* I received an additional, although possibly unnecessary, diagnosis of *Auditory Processing Disorder.* This was further confirmation that a genetic defect lay behind my speech and language difficulties.

I refer to the possibility of *APD* being an unnecessary additional diagnosis, because my problems in this area may already sit comfortably under the umbrella of autism. But, at least, through the lengthy *APD* diagnostic process, I gained some useful insight into the disabling nature of my speech and language difficulties.

It's unlikely that I will ever truly master the art of conversation. I can only hope that one day I will simply stop caring about whether I've strayed from the topic, or said something stupid, inappropriate or boring.

Perhaps, someday, ignorance really will become bliss.

## 41

## HUGO: 2005

*I've come to the conclusion, that for all of our carefully laid plans and intended goals, the most significant moments on the road to success appear out of nowhere—the result of some random shuffling of unexpected events.*

I first met *Hugo the harmonica player* during a recording session at my studio in Finsbury Park. He was a thirty-something, well-spoken individual with the confident glow of a professional man who did more for a living than earn a few pounds here and there playing the blues.

It turns out that not only was Hugo a decent harmonica player, he was also creative director of a leading advertising agency.

This, he revealed during a tea break in which I

proceeded to explain—at great length—why I thought advertising was a complete waste of time.

'All of those annoying TV commercials and billboards could never persuade *me* to buy a product,' I protested with perhaps a little too much vigour. Hugo, who obviously did not agree with my opinion simply smiled, and with the quiet contentment of a man on a £140,000 salary, packed away his silver harmonica, and handed me a fifty pound note for the two hours of studio time.

The following week, my *busy* schedule was rudely interrupted by the sound of a brick sized *Nokia*…

'Hi, is that Steve? It's Hugo, you know… the harmonica guy from the other day.'

'Ah yes, Hugo, good to hear from you,' I replied —hoping the unexpected phone call would result in another fifty-pound job.

But this was *not* why Hugo had called. Now, in his more usual guise as the high flying creative director of one of the UK's leading agencies, he was offering me something much bigger, and infinitely more lucrative.

'Look, Steve, we urgently need some music for a radio advert, are you up for producing it?'

'*Err… yes, sure, why not!*' I replied—not quite knowing exactly what I was saying *yes* to.

'Problem is, we need it… like… yesterday,*,*' he continued—as if *yesterday* hadn't happened yet.

I held the phone next to my diary and flicked loudly through its empty pages.

'Well, it'll be *tight* Hugo... but I think I can reschedule a few jobs and squeeze you in.'

'Great!' said a naively confident Hugo.

I suggest, in a crude approximation of advertising-speak, that he, '*shoots me over an email, and we can touch base once I've analysed the brief.*'

Hugo seemed to understand what I meant, so I concluded that I must have done a good job of instantly mastering the *lingo* of an industry I knew nothing about.

This was going surprisingly well.

The agency's client in this instance was a leading canned food producer. And *my* job was to come up with a soundtrack to help promote their new variation of *Big Chunky Soup*—a can of hot, meaty goodness, guaranteed to warm the extremities of one's anatomy on cold, winter nights.

The brief from Hugo was simple, keep it *cheesy*, inoffensive, and twenty-eight seconds long. Something suitable for a daytime audience of bored, soup-buying domestic goddesses. No stereotypes *here,* I thought.

The previous week I had tried to convince Hugo that *advertising is immoral, and really doesn't work anyway.* This week I was a passionate believer in the art of persuading an unwilling public to buy products they didn't need with money they probably didn't have.

It was like selling one's soul to the devil at the crossroads, at midnight, in exchange for some quick cash.

Where had my morals suddenly disappeared to? I pondered momentarily, and what would *Neil Young* have done if he were in my position? Probably the same thing I expect.

I also needed a change from the daily churn of hopelessly out of tune singers who were now hiring my studio to record their demo CDs. Inspired, no doubt, by that new Saturday night phenomenon—*The X-factor*. Thank you *Simon Cowell.*

## Asking For Money

The thing I hate most about working freelance is the part when a client asks, 'so, how much do you charge?'

I become acutely embarrassed, and awkward, and invariably talk myself *down* until we arrive at a price low enough to match my equally diminished self-esteem.

So when Hugo asks, 'how much do you charge?' I waffle on for ages about my policy of never over-charging, and building long-term relationships with clients, and how difficult it is to put a price on *art*. Anything, in fact, to avoid making a decision.

Then Hugo asks again. This time in a tone that appears to reflect a degree of annoyance: *'YES, STEVE…* but how much do you charge?'

'Well, Hugo,' I reply—further testing his patience. 'It really depends…'

'IT REALLY DEPENDS ON WHAT*?'* Hugo responds, with a heavy expulsion of exasperated breath. 'Can't you just give me a bloody number…?'

The negotiations are brought to a cringe-worthy close when Hugo suggests a fee of £1000, to which I instantly agree.

I hang up the phone and spend a few minutes frantically pacing across the studio floor whilst waving my arms around. This calms me down for a while, and I call Bonnie to tell her the good news.

Sixteen-hours later, the twenty-eight second masterpiece was finished.

*'Perfect,* that's just what we wanted,*'* said Hugo from his office, as I held the phone against one of the studio's powerful loudspeakers.

I arrived home somewhere around 9 am the following morning, and crawled into bed, exhausted, yet elated.

Suddenly, the phone rang on the bedside table. A quick glance at the clock informed me that I'd only been asleep for an hour.

'Hi Steve, it's Hugo, sorry to call you so early, I know you worked all night. But are you up for producing another one for the same (canned foods) company?'

'Yeah… sure,' I said—wondering why he couldn't have called me later on in the day.

'Problem is,' said Hugo, apologetically, and in words I was becoming accustomed to hearing, 'we need it… like… *yesterday*.'

With the promise of another £1000 for a day's work, I crawled out of bed, still half asleep, and made my way back to the studio.

Sometime later that evening, the second piece of music was finished.

'Sounds *great* Steve,' said a happy Hugo. 'Send in your invoice, and I'll make sure you get paid next week.'

Well, I thought, this is definitely *not* like the music industry…!

Somewhere around 4 am, and after only an hour's sleep in two days, I closed my eyes, and finally drifted off into reassuring dreams of shopping trolleys filled with cash, and a big warm belly on a cold, winter's day.

My induction into the world of advertising and marketing was swift. Within days of hearing my *Big Chunky Soup* commercial blaring from radios across the nation, another call came through…

'Hi, it's Hugo… we need you to come up with some music for a TV ad.'

'We need it… like, *yesterday*…?'

This time Hugo needed a bluesy-rock track for another of their clients—*Paramount Pictures.*

The job was to market a DVD box-set containing a range of their classic films:

*Forrest Gump, The Italian Job,* and *Grease* with John Travolta.

The relevant film clips were sent over to my studio by taxi, and for eighteen hours straight, *'RUN FORREST… RUN,'* and Michael Caine's, *'YOU'RE ONLY SUPPOSED TO BLOW THE BLOODY DOORS OFF!'* looped endlessly in my computer whilst I added drums, bass, keyboards, and guitar. And with the addition of a great harmonica solo from Hugo, the music was complete.

Once again, I emerged into the cool, pre-dawn air —tired, yet triumphant.

2005 had ended on a high for both my finances, and my new, unexpected career in advertising.

## 42

---

## IMPOSTER SYNDROME

*I dedicate this chapter to my best friend Dictaphone. May it's worn, and battered body rest in pieces.*

If impostor-syndrome were a medical condition, I would have been diagnosed with the severest case ever recorded.

My new career in advertising had taken me so far outside my comfort zone, I doubted whether I'd ever find my way back to safety. Hugo's confidence in my work had left me feeling flattered, but also a little confused.

'Why choose me?' I once asked him directly, 'there are loads of great producers out there.'

'It's simple,' he replied. 'Your work is great, and you always complete on time.'

Yet, as welcome as Hugo's encouraging words

were, they could not cure the incurable. They could not reverse my genetically acquired, non-existent, self-esteem.

With my position as the agency's music freelancer secured, Hugo often requested that I attend the agency's plush London headquarters whenever a job came in that required my involvement. I'd sit in on briefings and attempt uncomfortable small talk by the coffee-machine with my fellow *creatives*. But, I hated visiting his office. Each time my stomach would fill with the same species of butterfly that once ravaged my seven-year-old gut whenever Mr Williams dragged me back into class crying, and begging to go home.

Beyond the agency's lavish reception area lay uncharted, shark-infested waters. For me, this was a frightening world of intimidating executives in sharp suits, and trendy young designers—skilled in Photoshop, and knowing how to say exactly the right thing at exactly the right time. I possessed none of these desirable attributes, and would feel utterly out of place. Not, I hasten to add, that I ever feel *in-place* anywhere. But at the agency, my feelings of *out-of-place-ness* sometimes resulted in bouts of anxiety that would force me to hide behind a locked door in the men's bathroom at least once a day. I'd grit my teeth and venture back out into the office where I'd plough on into the night—long after most of the other *creatives* had left.

The following morning, and often after only two or three hours sleep, I'd be back at the agency bright and early to continue my work.

Having said good morning to the somewhat unfriendly receptionist with the three-inch, art-deco fingernails, I'd push through the swing doors, and into a large, open-plan office space. Everywhere, people that looked professional were doing things that looked incredibly important, and at the far end sat Hugo. His desk was the largest. He'd sit behind it like the world's busiest school teacher. Marking his subordinates creative outpourings for the new Budweiser *ad*, or asking why the wrong shade of *orange* had been used on a prototype Sainsbury's poster.

Everywhere, trendy young things were expertly manipulating artwork, and experimenting with text layouts on Apple Macs—their eyes looking up only to follow me on my long, slow motion walk from reception to Hugo's desk.

I may have mentioned elsewhere in this book, that whenever I'm overcome by self-consciousness and anxiety, I tend to lose track of where my limbs are in relation to their surroundings. I become awkward, and clumsy, and bump into things.

On one fairly typical occasion, I approached Hugo's desk. He was looking down at some artwork for a new *Sex and the City* project he wanted me to work on.

'Hi Hugo,' I said—bashing into the *unmissable*

bright yellow, swivel chair—sending it crashing into his desk with a loud bang.

The chair was now facing in the wrong direction, so I span it around to face him, and dropped down heavily onto the seat. This turned out to be a few inches lower than I'd expected.

'*OOOFF...*' I winced in shock.

'Sorry about that,' I said—realising that my office furniture *fail* had caused a wave of quizzical glares from above a number of glowing Apple Mac screens.

Hugo said nothing and smiled kindly. He must have known how uncomfortable I felt.

This was a few years before my autism diagnosis, and I'd had no idea it was common for people like *me* to be so socially awkward. I'd always assumed that my lack of *coolness* was due to either that thing people called me as a child—*abnormal*. Or, simply the over-abundance of stupidity genes handed to me at birth. It never occurred to me that my less-than-typical behaviour was actually *very* typical–in fact, entirely symptomatic of the developmental condition I'd soon become so acquainted with.

My biggest concern at the agency, however, was that people may think of me as: *Steve, the clumsy old guy that produces our music.*

I wanted to be: *Steve, the brilliant music guy— mature, yet still seriously cool.* The type of guy *everyone* in the creative team would want to be like when they grew up...

I could not, however, ignore the fact that I was a greying forty-something-year-old, clinically depressed, undiagnosed autistic—propped up by chocolate, caffeine and major depressive illness medication. And in addition to this, I had practically zero experience in the world of advertising. Yet, here I was, in the bosom of a top London agency's art department, discussing creative concepts I couldn't grasp, with fast talking, quick thinking young designers that spoke in sentences I couldn't begin to comprehend...

## My Best Friend Dictaphone

I'd sit with my fellow creatives in one of the obligatory glass-walled offices. There were white flip-chart boards covered with hand drawn, brain dump scribblings, and people drinking *Lattes* whilst thinking out of the box in blue-sky hats. To a man—yes, they were mostly men—my colleagues were slender twenty-something year-old, bearded-hipsters. They wore skinny jeans that would have been my size in 1976. But unlike me, circa 2006, they'd have little trouble taking a full breath of air without the buttons on their super-slim, figure-hugging shirts breaking free and pinging across the room.

Then Hugo begins to describe his concept on how to bring a new variety of salad cream to the attention of the masses.

'Sounds great *Hugo.* If we get it right, this Salad Cream could be *big,*' I'd remark—scouring my brain for every last morsel of believable optimism. After all, we were not just talking *Salad Cream* here. We were offering the people of Britain a paradigm shift in the way they ate their lettuce—it was *that* important.

Sometimes, in these meetings, I'd grasp just enough information to understand what was required of me. But all too often, my differently thinking, sieve-like brain would filter out all the relevant information, and allow all the superfluous stuff to leave me with an entirely wrong mental picture.

It was clear that I would need a little extra help to remember things. So, for my birthday, Bonnie bought me a small, digital Dictaphone. This would be hidden in my shirt pocket in record mode before entering a meeting. I would later listen back to the audio and make notes.

On listening back, I was frequently astounded by how often my contributions to the discussion were met by an embarrassing silence…

'Err, *no,* Steve,' Hugo would say. 'You've got the wrong idea. I thought we agreed an hour ago *not* to go with the little black dress idea for the Sex and the City promo...'

And yet another embarrassing meeting would end with a confidence crushing flashback to my primary school days. When, once again, I would be the only child in the room that didn't appear to *get it*…

## 43

# STEVE THE VIDEO GUY: 2006

*Although I was scared, I swam out to the edge of my comfort zone to where I could no longer feel the ground beneath my feet. And then out into the deeper waters beyond...*

The phone rang—it was Carlos.

'Hey *man*, how you *doin* bro?'

Carlos was a relatively well known Cuban rap artist who frequently recorded at my studio. I'd struggle to understand Carlos. The combination of his thick Spanish accent, and my inability to process even perfectly formed Queen's English, meant that we often talked at cross purposes. Graciously, Carlos would apologise for any misunderstanding—blaming it on his poor English language skills. Shamelessly, I would play on those few seconds of false superiority and offer a sympathetic: 'Never mind *Carlos,* you'll get the hang of it soon.'

I liked Carlos, he was everything I admired in a client—friendly, easy to please, reliable, and a good *payer*. One day he called to ask if I knew anyone that could make a music video for his new single. All of a sudden I heard myself saying, 'yes, *me… I'll* do it… and for a very reasonable price!'

By chance, I'd recently began to dabble in some video editing, and had even been paid for a couple of jobs, but I'd never *shot* a music video before. In fact, I'd never actually shot a video of *any* kind before. Not unless I include the time I borrowed dad's little video camera to film my daughter's fifth birthday party. Well, I say *film* my daughter's birthday party, what I actually captured was the floor, the ceiling, and a few shaky minutes of candles being blown out on what may have been a chocolate cake in an earthquake—I can't say for sure. All I knew was that I needed the money, and my friend *Andrew* was an experienced professional working in film and TV. *He'd* help me out if I needed some advice. And so began my new career behind the lens.

It was a scorchingly hot day in London's famous Portobello Road market. The bustling magnet for antique dealers and bric-à-brac stalls had been a popular destination for as long as anyone could remember. And before the slow creep of gentrification began to swallow up the surrounding streets, the large, semi-derelict properties had provided cheap housing for the thousands of West Indian immigrants arriving to help rebuild Britain after the second world war. But now, many of these houses had become investment vehicles for secretive foreigners with deep pockets and dirty cash. Yet, despite this, Portobello Road—historic home of the Notting Hill Carnival— had never entirely lost its Caribbean *soul*. By any standards, a summer's day in Portobello Road will always provide the perfect backdrop for a Cuban style music video.

*'ROLL PLAYBACK… AND… ACTION!'* I called loudly to the small crew of music video participants.

I'd never said these words before, and as they left my mouth they sounded foreign and pretentious—as if someone *else* should be saying them. Someone that actually knew what the hell they were doing. I wasn't even sure if I was using the correct terminology. Perhaps I should be saying *READY-STEADY-GO!* Or *321 BLAST OFF* instead?

But, no, *ROLL PLAYBACK… AND… ACTION* appeared to trigger the correct response from everyone involved. Instantly, the scene on the other side of the lens sprang into life—the powerful ghetto blaster sending hard Cuban beats echoing from every sun-baked, graffiti covered building. Either side of the rapping *Carlos*, scantily clad black women danced in ways that, in any other part of town, would have probably breached the rules on public decency. Fortunately, the growing band of male onlookers were enjoying the spectacle *far* too much to inform the police of this X-rated *Reggaeton* extravaganza.

'*CUT*,' I shouted… '*CUT*.'

'CARLOS—YOU NEED TO INTERACT MORE WITH THE DANCERS.'

'OK, LET'S DO ANOTHER TAKE.'

'Quiet on set… *QUIET ON SET*,' I repeated loudly, like an irritated school teacher regaining control over a disruptive class of noisy teenagers. 'ROLL PLAYBACK… AND… ACTION…'

Until it became too dark to film, we moved from one sun-drenched location to the next—collecting followers as though we were some sort of happy Carnival cult.

A week or so later the edit was complete, and Carlos was over-the-moon with the result. I must admit, it certainly captured the magic of that hot day in West London. And thanks to Carlos, it was not long before the phone began to ring with more enquiries from people with heavy Spanish accents…

'Hey Steve… *bro*… I got your number from

Carlos… he says *you're the man.* Can you make a video for my company?'

Within months, I had, accidentally, become the *go to* man for every Cuban in town requiring a video. The word continued to spread, and soon I was producing *Salsa* tuition videos for award-winning dance teachers, and filming Latin music festivals where thousands of people from around the world would congregate, to sample a heady dose of Cuban culture.

For years, the deafening sound of doors slamming shut at every turn had made me question my very existence. But venturing outside my comfort zone had created opportunities way beyond anything I could have imagined. Finally, I began to feel as though I were becoming an adult—taking control, forging my own path, making good decisions. And the interesting thing *was,* that none of this had anything to do with writing songs, playing the guitar or producing records. Perhaps I'd been chasing success in the wrong career all along...?

Some Months Later

It's 5 am, and I'm on the *Eurostar* train from London St Pancras.

Destination—Paris, France.

Mission—my first advertising video for a multinational company that's famous for manufacturing high quality yoghurt products.

On the seat opposite me is creative director *Hugo*, and the marketing lady from the yoghurt company.

My job is to film some *head shots* in Paris, create some animated yoghurt pots, add some titles, and edit everything into an exciting promotional video for a product that claims to, '*fix your skin... from within.*'

But the dirty little secret hiding under my ill-fitting Spielberg cap on that stressful journey to Paris, was that I hadn't actually filmed a corporate video before. Only hours, and hours of barely dressed Cuban dancers thrusting their sparkly bits at me and my camera lens. Hugo didn't know this, and neither did the marketing lady from the yoghurt company.

And as our train raced through the Channel Tunnel towards Paris, my anxiety became so intense, that I even contemplated leaping from the speeding vehicle into the first body of still water that came within jumping distance. I would catch a ferry back to England, whereupon I'd change my phone number, my address, and possibly even my identity—just in case Hugo decided to track me down in anger.

But then, suddenly, and in a rare moment of blinding insight, a defiant thought crossed my mind: *What's the worst thing that can possibly happen? SO WHAT if I screw up the video? SO WHAT if I forget to hit the record button on the camera and return to London with a blank tape?*

*YEAH,* SO WHAT...?

It's not like I'd be sent to prison, or burn in hell-fire for all eternity. The worst thing that could happen, was that Hugo would be angry with me, and give me the sack. I could live with that…

On the other hand. If I did a good job on the Paris shoot, he'd give me loads more video work, and I'd make a ton of money. Suddenly my anxiety levels dropped to manageable levels. I even began to relax, and attempted a little casual small talk with the power dressed marketing lady from the yoghurt company.

'Going anywhere nice for Christmas?' I asked. She didn't answer.

Hugo glared angrily at me as if to say, *'SHUT UP… can't you see, we're busy discussing a new £250,000 campaign?!'*

*Damn*, I thought—feeling stupid again. I just can't seem to get the hang of this small-talk stuff.

I spent the rest of the journey silently staring out of the window, knowing that as long as I didn't try to get too clever with all of those complicated video camera buttons, I may just get through this without being *found out.*

Finally, we arrived in Paris. It was cold and wet—much like London, but cleaner. Then, after a slap-up, all expenses paid lunch, we caught a taxi to the yoghurt company's grand, marble-floored headquarters. We filmed a few simple interviews, and caught the Eurostar back to London. The only embarrassing *rookie* moment came right at the end of the shoot when I couldn't work out how to fold the heavy metal tripod back into its case. We all laughed it off by agreeing, philosophically, that life was just so *damn* unnecessarily complicated these days.

On the journey back to London later that evening, I watched the French countryside race past the train window. I felt like a victorious Richard The Lionheart returning home from a glorious foreign crusade. My weapons of war resting proudly beside me in silver flight cases, until called upon to fight the next mighty battle.

A few weeks later, Hugo and I are on a business class flight to Brussels. Once again, cameras and tripods are my only luggage.

Everyone had been so delighted with the French video, that I was asked to film another one in Belgium. This time, however, I was prepared, and made light work of the shoot.

Within a year or two, my CV included Heinz, ASDA, GlaxoSmithKline, Disney-Pixar, Sex and the City, Waterstones, The Hard Rock Café, Unilever, Danone and many more.

Yet, still, I could not escape another relentless slide into clinical depression. The doctor, who was fast running out of ideas, added some powerful antipsychotics to my existing medication. But they only made me put on weight and feel constantly tired. I even began to hope the phone *wouldn't* ring, with Hugo offering me another amazing opportunity to advance my career, whilst adding substantially to my bank balance.

The drugs were definitely *not* working for me, and I was convinced that something else lay behind my mental health problems—some unknown factor that lurked far beyond the reach of those healing chemicals: *Zoloft*, *Olanzapine* and *Risperidone*.

'Why is my brain so slow?' I'd frequently ask my glassy-eyed, shoulder-shrugging doctor.

'Can I at least have a brain scan to find out why this is? Or how about giving me that new thing they surgically implant in depressed people's brains in America? Can't I have *that*?' I'd ask…

I began to feel like the annoying five-year-old on the back seat with an incessant need to know *whether we were there* yet. After a while everyone simply stops listening.

Soon I *would* discover the answers I'd been searching for my whole life, but not until the wheels had come off the *crazy* bus in a way they never had before.

## 44

## LOST IN TRANSLATION.

My wonderfully insightful daughter *Sophie* once remarked, 'I really wish *people* came with instructions.'

Personally, I wish people came with a forty-page training manual, and a comprehensive set of online video guides.

I generally find people confusing, intimidating, strange, and of a species wholly different to mine.

Interestingly, however, I draw a clear distinction between interactions that are work-based, and those that are purely social. The very nature of my work means that I am frequently in creative meetings with clients, discussing projects. This, for some reason, I can do quite well. Often, they are seeking advice, and I am offering it. This type of interaction has clearly defined goals. But the moment a client suggests we meet up for a drink after work sometime, my well-practised routine of plausible excuses are triggered.

So, when *Hugo* invited me to his wedding in Tuscany, I was—all at once—flattered, embarrassed and terrified.

I hadn't realised that not only did Hugo consider me a valuable addition to the creative department, he also saw me as a friend, worthy of an invitation to witness his big day in Central Italy. Unfortunately, this was an invitation I rejected in a way I can only describe as *badly*...

'Err, thanks, Hugo... but umm... I think we may have other arrangements *that* weekend...' I stutter embarrassingly.

'But I haven't told you which weekend it is yet...!' Replies an already offended Hugo.

'Umm... I'm sorry Hugo... we'd love to accept your invitation but... well... I think we're busy *all* the weekends this year...'

Such was the look of disappointment on Hugo's snubbed face, I knew our amicable working relationship could never be the same again. And for once, my instinct was correct. Gradually the offers of work slowed to a stop, and in 2010, my five-year career in advertising drew to an uneasy close with promotional video's for Disney-Pixar, Orange Mobile, Waterstones and yet more probiotic spinning yoghurt pot animations for the product still claiming it could *heal one's skin—from within*...

Sometime ago, I read in *Campaign Magazine* that Hugo had joined another agency as creative director. I'd like to meet up with him again one day to set the record straight. I always felt we parted on uncomfortable terms. I never did get round to thanking him for believing in me more than I ever believed in *myself.*

## 45

## THE DIAGNOSIS: 2008

Great aunt Anita was Grandpa's younger sister. She remembered the *old* days, just after the time our family came to England.

I hadn't spoken to her for a while, and it was good to catch up. But after we'd dispensed with the pleasantries, she turned the conversation towards the thorny, and usually out-of-bounds subject of my childhood.

'You had a lot of problems as a child *Steven*. The doctors told your mum you'd end up in an institution, and you'd probably never come out—she was very worried about you.'

Aunt Anita continued…

'You were terrified of people coming to the house, and would run and hide whenever the doorbell rang. You hated any type of change to your routine, and you rarely played with other children. In fact, I always thought you were *autistic*.'

Suddenly, I remembered how the sound of the doorbell made me jump out of my skin—as if a bomb had exploded in my nervous system—sending shock waves cascading throughout my body. I remembered running full speed up the single flight of carpeted stairs to the safety of my bedroom, where I'd hide until the visitor had left.

Then I realised that I'm *still* scared of the doorbell, and the painful rush of panic whenever it rings. And how I hate opening the front door to strangers—uncertain of how the interaction will go.

But it's not only doorbells that throw me into an uncontrollable internal spin. It's *any* sudden loud noise. Like when Bonnie releases one of her thunderous sneezes. I can just about handle *one* of these at close quarters without running from the room holding my ears, but then, she'll sneeze again, and again in rapid succession without allowing me to recover between each catastrophic nasal explosion. Then the dog will bark, the alarm will go off on the cooker, the postman pushes that dreaded doorbell and the phone will ring with uncaring intensity, my senses are thrown upside down and inside out as adrenaline pumps through my body in rippling shock waves. I run upstairs to the quiet of our bedroom, where I close my eyes and turn off for a while—just as the child did that aunt Anita had described.

Within minutes of ending our conversation, I was on the computer typing the word *autism* into the Google search bar. I quickly came across dozens of case studies, and realised that my own story would sit quite happily amongst them.

Could aunt Anita be right? Was autism the unexplainable *something* I'd been searching for my entire adult life?

Two days after the conversation with my ageing relative, I sat opposite my new psychologist. This was the first time I'd met *Dr C*—as I shall call her. She is an affable, thirty-something year old woman, with long mousy-coloured hair and an easy-going personality.

This was to be the first of six, weekly Cognitive Behavioural Therapy sessions. I'd not tried this form of therapy before, and was, if I'm completely honest, more than a little doubtful as to whether it could cure my, as yet, incurable depression.

'*So... tell me about your childhood, Steven,*' the *young doctor* asked.

I took a long, deep breath and rolled my eyes.

By the age of forty-eight, *my childhood* was a story I'd told a thousand times to a thousand different therapists, psychologists, GP's and psychiatrists— none of whom had been able to explain the persistent symptoms that seemed to fall beyond the diagnostic scope of my mental health disorders.

Dr C listened patiently until I'd finished my well told story, and then calmly asked:

'Has anyone ever mentioned the words *High Functioning Autism* to you before?'

'*No,* doctor,' I replied—quickly adjusting my answer to, 'well, actually, yes, just a couple of days ago, a relation told me that she'd always thought I was autistic!'

'Well, in my opinion,' continued Dr C. 'You either have some type of brain damage, or you're autistic. Perhaps we should put the Cognitive Behavioural Therapy on hold for a few weeks and get you tested for autism…'

I left Dr C's office, and adjourned to a nearby café to ponder the consequences of what she'd said…

But surely, I thought, If I really *did* have autism, how come I wasn't severely disabled like the children I once worked with as a volunteer for MENCAP? Or the stereotypical computer nerd living in the basement of his parent's house without a friend in the world?

But then I remembered that Dr C had also explained that autism is a kind of spectrum condition, and that everyone on it is likely to display their symptoms differently.

She'd said that some autistic people are able to live independently, get married, have children, and sustain successful careers, whilst others have additional learning difficulties, and will need constant one to one support for the rest of their lives. But wherever a person falls on the spectrum, they will have deficiencies in their social and communication skills, along with sensory, and information processing difficulties.

And *that* was when the autistic penny finally dropped. Dr C had described my entire forty-eight-year battle with life, the universe and everything contained within it.

I gazed out through the café window and sipped my white, unsugared Americano, hoping that Dr C's assumptions would amount to something more than just another false, and disheartening dawn…

The process of diagnosing autism is neither quick, or straightforward. There are a number of lengthy practical tests to gauge a person's general cognitive ability, their short and long term memory, their speech and language processing skills, their social imagination, and emotional reciprocity. This tiresome process can be made even *more* difficult if the patient has an existing mental health condition such as OCD, social anxiety or severe clinical depression. And also if the patient has a specific learning difficulty such as dyslexia, or ADHD, or a more significant global learning delay.

However, the part of the diagnostic process I was looking forward to the least, was the part where Dr C would interview my mother to get a full developmental history.

But first, I had to break the embarrassing news to mum that she would be receiving a call from my psychologist.

'Hi mum, it's me, err, yeah… I'm fine, thanks. You remember how I had all those problems when I was a kid? Well, you'll never guess what the doctor has just told me? She thinks I'm autistic! Yeah… I know… she must be crazy—*me autistic,* I'm not even a child! Look, mum, would you mind having a quick chat with her on the phone sometime, y'know, just to rule it out…?'

During my next appointment with Dr C, she mentioned the hour-long conversation she'd had with mum the previous week...

'She's got a good memory, your mum. She told me everything…'

*That you didn't speak until you were six. The doctors at the children's hospital said you were probably Schizophrenic, and gave you Lithium. You hated change, you never slept or ate. They said you'd be locked up in an institution and would never come out. You would read three books at the same time, you hated people and would spend every moment alone. You'd (ritualistically) bang your head on the floor, rock backwards and forward, and walk around in circles humming. Your parents didn't think you'd have a future… No one knew what was wrong with you…!*

Dr C had heard enough and was ready to conclude her investigations.

'Well, Steven, you definitely meet the criteria for a diagnosis of autism,' announced Dr C with a reassuring confidence. 'And because of your speech problems as a child, I have decided on a diagnosis of autism as opposed to Asperger Syndrome.'

Instantly, I wanted to know *everything,* and, in detailed, unassailable, triplicate. 'Does that mean I'm *autistic*—are you sure? Are you absolutely sure *Dr?* So… You're saying I have A*utism*, *High Functioning Autism…* I'm on the autistic spectrum? Do you think I've *always* had it? Or do you think it's only come on recently?'

I battered the poor doctor with a lifetime of unanswered questions—each one responded to in the affirmative, by a professional, completely satisfied with her conclusion.

I left the smiling Dr C's office with one final piece of advice—'STOP GOOGLING THE WORD *AUTISM*, STEVEN, YOU'RE BECOMING OBSESSED…!'

I stepped out onto a crowded London street in a way I never had before. I was *new,* and everything around me felt open to a fresh interpretation. I wanted to shout loudly to the rush hour traffic: *'I'M NOT STUPID AFTER ALL… JUST DIFFERENT—NOT WRONG, JUST AUTISTIC…!'*

To say that Dr C changed my life is an understatement of near biblical proportions. Things had begun to make sense. But I knew this was only the beginning of life re-observed through the lens of my wondrous new perspective.

Never again would I resist the urge to cover my ears when a police car raced past with its siren wailing, and no longer would I worry about asking someone to repeat an instruction *slowly,* so that I could understand what they meant. And as for the collection of plausible excuses I'd use to avoid social events, well, I wouldn't need those any longer. Everyone knows that autistic people struggle *socially.*

This was day one of learning how to be *me,* the autistic *me*—out and proud, and free from the pressure of conforming to anyone else's concept of normality.

## After The Diagnosis

I'm not *exactly* sure what I thought would happen after the diagnosis, but I definitely expected *something…*

I thought, perhaps, at the very least, a range of autism support services would become available to, well, you know, help me make sense of things.

I waited… and waited some more… but all was strangely quiet on the clinical front. Nothing but a few lonely crickets chirping in a barren autistic desert. Maybe—I thought, optimistically—all the relevant professionals were on holiday. Or busy in the halls of medicine dreaming up some all encompassing plan of action. The type rolled out to *all* new recipients of an autism diagnosis.

Feeling more than a little deflated, and wondering what, if anything, I should do next, I approached my local doctor for advice, and to gain some clarity on the plan *going forward*.

'Err… what plan was that then *Steven*?' Replied Dr Winters (not her real name) with a quizzical glaze smeared across her face.

'Well, you know, doctor, the plan where I get access to all of those autism support services?'

'Which services exactly were you thinking of?' She replied with bemused irritation.

I continued on in earnest.

'*You* know, doctor? Autism *therapy*… treatment… cures… support—that sort of thing?'

'Hmm…' offered Dr Winters—apparently beaten in our frustrating little game of verbal tennis.

She leaned back in her chair and folded her arms —this, I am told, means that someone no longer wants to talk to you.

'Well *Steven*, there *is* no *next* as such, have you

looked for information on the internet…?' My heart sunk.

She may as well have said: '*Well, you've got your diagnosis, Jack… go figure it out for yourself, and don't bother me again!*'

I took the hint, and left her office feeling utterly dejected.

On my way out through reception, I passed rows of lucky, easy-to-fix patients who will probably get better in a week or two with a dose of antibiotics, or a dab of ointment for some ghastly rash in some unmentionable place. If only I *too* could have emerged from Dr Winter's office with a squeezy tube of autism-cream, or even a drop of hope that I may be referred somewhere to learn how to move forward in my new autistic world.

And so began my research into this sometimes wonderful, often challenging, but always enigmatic condition called autism.

My initial internet searches revealed a distinct lack of information relating to the more *mature* person on the spectrum.

In fact, the casual observer could have easily concluded that autistic children become neurotypical the moment they pass their eighteenth birthday. This, as we know, is untrue. So why exactly *wasn't* anyone talking about the problems *older* autistic's face in the workplace, in their relationships, and with their mental health? Where could I read about stuff that related to *me*?

Surely there must be others with my brand of autism—the type I describe as, just enough ASD to turn the simplest of everyday tasks into the mightiest of undertakings, or, just enough ASD to make me think *differently,* even when I try really, *really* hard not to…

So, in 2010, I launched the self-help website *adultswithautism.org.uk.*

Within months, my inbox was awash with messages from desperate autistic adults, and with stories that sounded, sadly, all too familiar…

*'Hi Steve… I'm fifty-two years of age, and your article has summed up my entire life. I've always felt as though I were different. I haven't worked for years, and feel so depressed. Can you give me some advice?'*

Others said…

*'I'm thirty-seven, and can relate to everything you wrote about undiagnosed autism. But, my doctor doesn't understand, and refuses to refer me for a diagnosis, please help…'*

And…

*'Help!… My daughter has just been diagnosed with Asperger Syndrome, and this has made me realize that I am also autistic, but my doctor said it only happens to children… What can I do?'*

It was clear that most autistic adults felt isolated, marginalised, and helpless. They looked to *me* for answers, but at the time I was far from being an *expert* on the subject. All I could do was write about my own experiences, and hope that others would feel comforted in some way.

*Adultswithautism.org.uk* has grown tremendously over the past few years. It has attracted opportunities for me to speak at conferences, guest on national radio, and advise the police on how to communicate more effectively with people on the spectrum. The website keeps me pretty busy these days—as do the many films I still make for various organisations.

It's been ten years—at the time of writing—since autism became the prominent word in my vocabulary. And to adequately describe how my life has changed as a result, would fill an entire second book—now there's an interesting idea?

Note to diary—*write another book.*

But hang on, I'm not quite finished with *this* one yet. I haven't spoken about my revised theory on what it means to be *normal,* or indeed *abnormal*—a word that has haunted me for the past fifty years. And, I haven't told you about the other life changing events that made 2008 such a transformational year.

So, without further ado, I shall refer you to the following chapter...

## 46

---

## 2008

2008 was memorable for several life-changing reasons. It was the year I gave up on the music business, and the year my depression became so intense I didn't think I'd make it through till Christmas. It was the year my mother passed away, and the year I was diagnosed with autism.

January began much the way December had ended. A continuous slide into mental illness and business debt, each feeding off the other's darkness in a hellish race to the bottom.

Some days, the medication would render me unable to link one thought to the next. Yet still somehow, I'd show up at my recording studio each morning to battle the opposing forces of ambition and depression. Some days all I could do was sleep, deeply, in that creaky old swivel chair. My feet resting on the redundant mixing desk that once channelled such immense creativity and hope. I'd wake into the electronic hum of expectant sound equipment in that half lit space, and self-medicate with gallons of strong coffee and chocolate.

Somehow, I'd find the strength to compose a few bars of music for a *Hard Rock Cafe* commercial, or animate the graphics for a toothpaste advert. And then I'd sleep again for an hour or two to clear my tired, chaotic thoughts.

And so the daily descending spiral continued. Week after hopeless week until all resolve was gone.


## August: 2008

'It's got to go… it's all got to go.'

I stood at the door of my dark basement recording studio and scowled into the room as though addressing an abusive partner in a dysfunctional relationship.

'I hate you, and I cannot be here any longer. I'm sick of your grubby white walls and your coffee-stained carpets. You smell like death. That's it we're finished…'

I reached for the phone and called the landlord to tell him I was giving up music and no longer wanted to rent the space.

Obligingly, he agreed to end our agreement with immediate effect, but on the condition that I empty the building of equipment within two days, so he could move another tenant in as soon as possible.

The purge began within minutes—carload after carload until the building was empty.

Into the deep, recycling containers—already partially filled with broken furniture—my once beloved recording studio equipment disappeared with the deafening clang of engineered metal on metal. A dissonant final symphony that echoed throughout the vast underground disposal centre.

I returned briefly to the now empty studio space to check I hadn't left anything behind. Then, leaving my key on the side, I turned and walked away.

The purge was complete, and I was free. I wanted to call mum, to tell her I'd given up music, and had closed the studio down, but this was not a conversation we could ever have…

September: 2008

My final Sunday afternoon visit to mum's hospice was little more than an exercise in self-torture through endless reminiscence.

Every bone in my body ached with uncried tears and the expectation of inevitable, irreversible change. Mum's battle with cancer was all but lost and the day's of hope for some miracle recovery were gone.

Unable to take any more painful reflection, I left mums bedside and walked out into the crisp, late

September evening knowing this would be our final sunset together.

'Goodnight mum,' I whispered to the gold and purple sky.

'Safe journey…'

## 47

# WHAT IS NORMAL ANYWAY?

For the record, I would like to say that I'm not a big fan of the word *autistic*. Not that there's anything particularly wrong with the term. After all, it's what we are—*autistic*. There's just something about the word that makes me cringe with embarrassment every time I hear it, or describe myself *as* it. I think it's the '*istic*' part of the word that takes me back to my childhood, and the hospital ward where I first heard doctors refer to physically disabled children as *spastic*, and children like me, as *retarded*, *disturbed* and *maladjusted*.

Then there's the language people in the autism community use to describe themselves. There are many opposing views on this hotly debated topic. Are we *autistic,* or people with *autism?* Perhaps we are simply individuals that have ASD*?*

Others say that labels really do not matter anyway,

and that we should stop obsessing over words. But then, asking an autistic person to stop obsessing is like telling a frog not to croak.

I've followed many-a-heated online debate on the *autistic-autism* question. Some people have become so entrenched in their opinion, they've even resorted to threats of violence against anyone who uses opposing variations of autism terminology.

With a degree of irony, and perhaps a little humour, this display of poorly regulated emotion and inflexible thinking, shows just how *autistic* these online commentators actually are.

And to add another spanner into the already complicated autism works, in the latest diagnostic guidelines—*the DSM-5*—Asperger Syndrome is no longer specified. Therefore, there will be no new *aspies*. Just lots of people with *ASD*.

In my opinion, this is a mixed blessing. I worry that in an attempt to simplify things, people with harder to spot autistic symptoms may slip through the diagnostic net and therefore not receive the support they need. I'm quite sure, however, that the gradually shifting sands of clinical thinking will produce further revisions to future versions of the diagnostic guidelines. Who knows, perhaps the term *Autism* will be scrapped altogether one day…?

My obsession with the concept of *normality* began in childhood, and more–or–less ends with the writing of this book.

You see, I think I *get* it now.

Until recently, I had assumed that every single citizen of this vast planet was, in fact, alarmingly *normal,* and it was only *I* that owned the contradictory classification of *not* being it. however, during my exhaustive quest to understand how I too can become *normal,* I have made some rather interesting discoveries.

It turns out that *normality* is a relative state of being—largely defined by culture and belief. And that, at any time, new versions of *normality* can be forced onto a population, by those with the loudest voices, and the greatest power.

But in the context of a discussion on autism, *normality* is largely judged on how we interact socially. Is our body language perceived as odd? And is our mode of communication consistent with what's considered typical?

Sometimes, when I've strayed outside of these social norms, a well-meaning neurotypical will try to make me feel better by saying, 'not to worry Steve, everyone's a *bit* autistic.' I respond by pointing out that it's not possible to be a *bit* autistic. You either meet the criteria or you do not. It's not simply about disliking crowds, or noisy places or bright lights. Autism is about so much *more* than that. It's the mighty disconnect that keeps me from engaging with my surroundings, the *social dyslexia* which prevents me from progressing in life, and the difficulty I have in processing speech and language. These things are neither *treatable* traits, or *me too* life choices.

I do not wear my autistic symptoms like temporary fashion statements to gain sympathy for my shortcomings. My autism is real. It's for life, and I cannot be *fixed*.

I can, however, learn to accept the way I am, and forgive myself for being *different*.

## Can Science Make Us Normal?

Did you know, there are scientists working in the field of autism research, who are determined to find a *cure* for the condition?

It's true. Right now, there will be a scientist somewhere, analysing the data from their latest attempt to reverse the symptoms of autism, so that, one day, I *too* can become *normal*.

I subscribe to a variety of autism research newsletters. They arrive in my Inbox each day with exclusive, attention grabbing headlines like…

*GENE THERAPY FOUND TO CURE AUTISM-LIKE SYMPTOMS IN MICE!* A recent study has shown that… *blah blah blah.*

And...

*BREAKING NEWS!* Scientists have confirmed the success of a new wonder-drug that prevented 90% of white rabbits flapping their paws in an autistic fashion whilst mating. A spokesman said that human trials will begin soon... (I jest, of course)

Whenever I see articles like these, a number of important questions come to mind. Firstly, when was it discovered that mice can have autism? And secondly, how is it that research into autistic rabbits gets more funding than research into autistic humans? On behalf of the autism community—I object... (again, I jest)

Thirdly, why isn't all of that precious money used for something more useful, like, finding a cure for cancer, or back pain, or sex therapy lessons for white autistic rabbits, or better still, support for dyslexic *Moles*. Surely the world would be a much better place if only those pesky little creatures could read the *KEEP OFF THE GRASS* signs. Perhaps then they'd stop digging holes in everyone's backyard...

Alternatively, can we not just accept that some people are a differently shaped peg to the hole that society has designed for them? I'm sure those clever scientists have my best interests at heart—and, of course, all of that research funding in their bank accounts. But even if there *were* a cure for autism, how exactly would it work?

Would fifty milligrams of *autism-fixing-medica-*

*tion* make me fifty per cent more neurotypical? And would this mean that I would begin to see the world fifty per cent less differently?

What if I decided to *really* go for it, and took a hundred milligram dose of the latest autism-fixing wonder-drug? Who would I become? And which variation of *normal* would I conform to? So many questions, and as usual, not nearly enough answers.

If those clever people in white-coats ever *do* come up with a cure for autism—the one that may have prevented *Einstein* from thinking differently enough to come up with all of that *Theory of Relativity* stuff. Or the one that may have prevented the great Temple Grandin from *thinking like a cow*—well, I think I'd have to say thanks, but no *thanks*. I prefer the alternative solution of learning how to become a happier version of the person I already am.

I will concede, however, that there are a few behavioural adjustments those of us on the spectrum could benefit from if adopted.

For example, when talking to someone at a party, don't stand too close. I recommend leaving a path wide enough for an obese forty-year-old male to squeeze by with a heaving plate of chocolate cake. If —after he's squeezed between *you*, and whoever you're talking with—you find brown skid marks on your new shirt, then either the hungry giant has forgotten the rules on personal space, or *you* have.

Another useful tip for a successful evening of fun

with friends, is to remember that other people may not necessarily share your passion for second-century Japanese cave-art—if, indeed, there *is* such a thing. Sometimes at social gatherings, *normal* people really *do* just want to talk about *normal* things, such as their recent, once-in-a-lifetime sightseeing trip to New York. You don't have to spoil their happy memories by relating your theory on why you think 9/11 was an inside job. Or asking whether they'd found it difficult to breathe with all of those cancerous Nano-thermite particles still floating around in the New York air.

When it comes to small talk, just remember that *simple* is usually best, and *less* is generally safer. Keep it light-hearted, smile a lot, and nod in agree-ment approximately every thirty-seconds, and you'll be fine…

*'Sounds fascinating… and how is the weather in New York this time of year,'* I enquire with just enough false interest to indicate that I'm nothing less than totally absorbed in their romantic trip to the Big Apple—when all I can *really* think about is how to end the conversation without appearing rude.

The influential entrepreneur and marketing guru, *Seth Godin*, talks about *finding your tribe*—that small group of true fans who will buy into your world-view. I think that as autistic people we can learn something from this idea. Some people will find my particular world view a little strange, and others will not. We just need to find *our tribe*—the people that can accept and love us for who we are.

We can never be *all* things to *all* people. But being *some* things to *some* people, *some* of the time, is usually good enough—*most* of the time.

## 48

## IN CONCLUSION

As I've previously discussed in the chapter entitled, *The Impossible Art of Conversation,* there are three aspects of a discussion I find particularly difficult— the start, all that stuff in the middle, and, of course, the *end*.

With this analogy in mind, I have reached the part of the book I compare to the end of a long, and some- what embarrassing conversation. It is now, therefore, time for the post-interaction analysis to begin…

Did I say too much? Not enough? Was I boring? Does anyone care what I think, anyway?

And, so, attempting to put paranoia, and social anxiety aside for a moment, I shall attempt to exit this long and self-indulgent discourse in a way that, I hope, will not leave me feeling incredibly guilty of some unimaginable crime.

And to further milk the—*having a conversation*

*with someone*—analogy, one final time, I begin to ponder the merits of ending with either a hilarious joke, or a mind-blowing piece of life-changing wisdom that is both unique, *and* utterly unassailable.

Alternatively, I could do that thing common in popular drama, of leaving *you* (*the reader*) in suspense, and needing to know what happened *next*. But, again, am I arrogant enough to believe that anyone really would care?

In this book, I've discussed at great length, my somewhat unusual journey from childhood, to wherever I am at present. But I'd like to think the bigger story is about overcoming adversity. It's about dragging oneself out of bed each morning in defiance of the fear and depression that tries to pull us back under those safe, warm covers. And, just how important it is for us, as autistic adults, to find a way of life that leads to fulfilment and happiness.

I leave you with just one last big, chewy thought-provoking statement on which to munch:

'Regardless of who you are, life will be good, bad, confusing, fulfilling, painful, enjoyable, exciting, boring, distressing and wonderful for eighty-something years, and then, finally, one day, the lights will go out…'

*Steven.*

## ACKNOWLEDGMENTS

I would like to thank my wife and daughters for their endless support, patience, and literary critique.

I would also like to thank…

Chick Corea, Pat Martino, Paul Desmond, John Coltrane, Miles Davis, Stan Getz and Bill Evans for the music that kept me sane throughout the writing of this book.

**Please consider leaving a review for this book on Amazon.**

Thanks Steve

Printed in Great Britain
by Amazon